Phenomenology
And Metaphysics

Phenomenology And Metaphysics

by

WILLIAM A. LUIJPEN, O.S.A., PH.D.

1965
Duquesne University Press, Pittsburgh, Pa.
Editions E. Nauwelaerts, Louvain

Library of Congress Catalog Card Number 65-13055

All rights reserved

© 1965 by DUQUESNE UNIVERSITY, Pittsburgh, Pa.

Produced in U.S.A., Computer Typesetting, Inc., Pittsburgh, Pa.

iv

TABLE OF CONTENTS

TABLE OF CONTENTS

vi

TABLE OF CONTENTS

PREFACE

In the realm of philosophy it is not possible to be an authentic thinker unless one allows tradition to play an inspiring role. The so-called "classical" works of the past embody the collective history of what mankind has "seen." Those works became classical precisely because their authors were first in giving verbal expression to a vision which no one else had "seen" before them. Such a seer often was like the voice of one crying in the desert. Only later, sometimes even only much later, others also began to "see" what he had "seen." What we and our contemporaries now "see" we always owe also to the efforts of what others have "seen" before us.

"Seeing," however, is a personal act. The original vision, the "seeing" that originated in the genius of a great thinker, has to be kept alive through the subsequent personal "seeing" of others. Human truth does not exist and live outside the personal and collective history of individual human beings who "see." It is possible, therefore, for human truth to die in the course of history.

Truth, however, never reveals itself as an absolute "light." Within the history of truth as encounter with reality truth allows itself to be "grasped" only as the chiaroscuro, the semi-darkness, of unconcealedness and concealedness. For this reason any act of "seeing" is at the same time an invitation to project a new "seeing." Those who fail to recognize this fact deprive truth of life because they cut it off from its future.

Thus it follows that the authentic character of thinking

cannot be safe-guarded if a philosopher is satisfied with endeavoring to preserve tradition. The very truth contained in tradition itself calls for a future. For, the preservation of truth is a human act which, precisely because it is human, cannot rigidly hold fast to any achieved result without becoming petrified in a kind of *rigor mortis*. In other words, although tradition is a source of inspiration, man's thinking becomes petrified if at the same time he is not also willing to go beyond tradition.

There is a second reason why rigid adherence to tradition dooms man's thinking to fruitlessness. One who swears by tradition, swears also by its mistakes, its extremisms, its inequalities of emphasis. More even than the petrifaction of its achievements, these mistakes, extremisms and inequalities of emphasis proper to any particular way of thinking, make human thought fruitless by depriving it of the possibility to extend its efforts to "everything." A philosophy becomes a failure not so much because of what it says as because of what it simply eliminates by speaking in a certain way. Such an elimination, however, cannot be made with impunity. "Reality" imposes itself, even when explicit thought does not want to "see." "To be unwilling to see" means here "to be *unable* to say explicitly what is 'surreptitiously,' implicitly, 'recognized'." The "primitive fact" or "central reference point," which makes a way of thinking a particular or specific way of thinking and which is found in any coherent system of thought, is the reason why a failing philosophy is *unable* to express certain aspects of reality. The fact that reality imposes the "surreptitious recognition" of these aspects is the reason why man at last will find it impossible to continue to speak explicitly in terms of that restricted way of thinking. The dialogue which the explicit thinking of the old restricted way has with reality is constantly thwarted by the "surreptitious recognition" of

the aspects of reality which explicit thought has eliminated. In such a situation the human mind can merely repeat "blindly" the customary replies to the questions of
the past. Its thinking is no longer able to achieve anything
worthwhile and has become fruitless.

All this applies also to the phase of philosophical reflection which is called "metaphysical" in the strict sense
of the term. In the Middle Ages, metaphysical thinking
had reached unparalleled heights. When, after the period
of positivism, European thought once again became interested in philosophy, and in existentialism and phenomenology attained results which for centuries had
been considered impossible, scholastic metaphysics remained behind. Undoubtedly, it profited by the renewed
interest in philosophical questions, but it did not succeed
in going beyond the repetition of former replies. As a
consequence of this failure, scholastic metaphysics remained a stranger to the crucial concerns of contemporary thinking. By simply taking up again the thread of
tradition and neglecting to rise at the same time above
this tradition, scholastic metaphysics cut itself off from
its own future. It became sterile.

That sterility manifests itself very clearly. On the one
hand, scholastic metaphysics continued simply to repeat the traditional replies; on the other, it has received
an added extension in its struggle against contemporary
thinking. Yet this struggle has not orientated it to a new
future, for its struggle against contemporary thinking
seeks all its inspiration in its own traditional answers
to its own traditional problems. This alone is enough
to make scholastic metaphysics sterile. In his own penetrating way Heidegger has paid attention to scholastic
metaphysics, but his efforts did not induce it to abandon
its negative attitude.

The purpose of this book is to investigate the cause of

the sterility affecting scholastic metaphysics and to disclose the mistake on which its negativism toward the contemporary thinking of existential phenomenology is based. In doing this, we will make constant use of Heidegger's ideas. Nevertheless, this work should not be regarded as a book *about* Heidegger, for, as in our previous works, we want to philosophize in a relatively autonomous way.

It would be wrong, however, to regard our critique of traditional metaphysics as purely negative and destructive. We are positively interested in traditional metaphysics and do not hesitate to affirm that it contains searching questions and answers which no other way of thinking metaphysically can propose with the same radicalism. Purified from objectionable elements through contact with contemporary thought, traditional metaphysics remains eminently worthy of man's attention in his never-ending quest of truth.

William A. Luijpen, O.S.A.

The translation of this book was made by the undersigned from the author's original manuscript and submitted to him for his personal approval. Subdivisions of chapters, as well as indexes of names and subject matter, have been added to facilitate orientation. German and French quotations in the footnotes have been retained because most of them are sufficiently paraphrased in the text itself.

Translations of Heidegger's work present a large variety of ways in which the German terms *Seiendes* and *Sein* are expressed. To retain the etymological connection, we have translated his *Sein* and the author's *zijn* by *being*, and *Seiendes* or *zijnde* by *be-ing*. Where the author used *Zijn* to refer to the Transcendent Being or God, we have used *Being*.

Duquesne University   Henry J. Koren, C.S. Sp.

CHAPTER ONE

THE METAPHYSICAL QUESTION

1. *Preliminary Considerations*

There was a time when many people considered themselves entitled to laugh at phenomenology because, so they said, there were as many phenomenologies as there were phenomenologists. The brief history of phenomenology, however, has already shown how premature these laughs were. The "many" phenomenologies have shown themselves possessed of a remarkable unity, whose force makes itself felt today in every realm of human thought.

What we have said here about phenomenology applies in a certain sense also to metaphysics. There are differences, of course. For instance, unlike phenomenology, metaphysics is of a venerable antiquity. In its case, however, there also have always been people who thought that they could laugh at metaphysics. They forgot and continue to forget that metaphysical thinking, despite all its difficulties, despite all the objections which it causes, and despite the many forms in which it manifests itself, reveals such a unity of inspiration that without a metaphysics it is not even possible to laugh at metaphysics.

Meaningfulness and Meaninglessness of the Question About Metaphysics

What, then, one will ask, is metaphysics? That question

1

should be preceded by another: Is it meaningful to try to say what metaphysics is? This question is often asked in our time, usually in a broader context, in connection with a reflection upon the character of philosophy in general. Is it meaningful to try to define philosophy?

There are several ways in which one can know what philosophy is. There is a way of speaking "about" philosophy which defines philosophy "from a standpoint lying outside philosophy itself."[1] Such a way of speaking embodies a superficial "knowledge" from without. Any speaking about philosophy which does not proceed from the pursuit of the essence of philosophy does not really penetrate into it and give authentic expression to its reality. Only in philosophizing itself does philosophy find its own essence and arrive at the same time at a kind of "knowledge" of this essence. The question of what philosophy is can be answered only philosophically.[2]

The same applies also to metaphysics. The attempt to define metaphysics from without cannot go together with the claim to arrive in this way at an authentic knowledge of what metaphysics is. Such a combination is a sterile undertaking.[3] It is only in metaphysical thinking itself that metaphysics discovers its own essence and arrives at a certain "knowledge" of this essence.[4]

There are limits, however, to the truth of what has been said here about what metaphysics is. For it is possible

---

[1] "Wenn wir fragen: Was ist das - die Philosophie ?, dann sprechen wir *über* die Philosophie. Indem wir auf diese Weise fragen, bleiben wir offenbar auf einem Standort oberhalb und d.h. ausserhalb der Philosophie." Heidegger, *Was ist das - die Philosophie* ? Pfullingen, 1960, p. 8.

[2] "Was ist das - die Philosophie ? Die Antwort kann nur eine philosophierende Antwort sein, eine Antwort, die als Ant-wort in sich philosophiert." Heidegger *ibid.*, p. 30.

[3] Heidegger, *Einführung in die Metaphysik,* Tübingen, 1953, p. 6.

[4] Heidegger, *ibid.*, pp. 15-17.

to indicate how the term "metaphysics" has been understood in the past. One who investigates that question does not claim to define metaphysics. True, he does not arrive at the authentic "knowing" which accompanies metaphysical thinking as an understanding of itself. Nevertheless, one cannot say that his efforts are necessarily fruitless. One who investigates how the term "metaphysics" has been used in the past discovers a unity of inspiration, which explains why a certain way of thinking is called "metaphysical" while others are not considered to be metaphysical. He will discover also that contemporary thinking must satisfy certain conditions if it wants to lay claim to being metaphysical.[5]

As soon, however, as one pays attention to the unity of inspiration which characterizes all metaphysical thinking, one discovers also that even the anti-metaphysicians are nourished by the same inspiration. Without metaphysics it is not possible to reject metaphysics. This is the reason why historical studies of metaphysics can conveniently place metaphysicians and anti-metaphysicians side by side.

In his later years, Heidegger himself has begun to reject the qualifier "metaphysical" with respect to his thinking. He regards his own thinking as a "transcending of metaphysics" so that it would no longer be metaphysical. By "transcending metaphysics," he tries to bring about the destruction of traditional metaphysics. Nevertheless, Heidegger's work reveals the same unity of inspiration, and he himself seems to be aware of this.[6]

---

[5] "So ist nur im Hinblick auf das, was Metaphysik vom Ursprung bei Parmenides bis zu ihrem Ende bei Hegel in einer inneren Einheit war, auszumachen, was sie ist und sein kann." L. Landgrebe, *Der Weg der Phänomenologie,* Gütersloh, 1963, pp. 76-77.

[6] "Negierend verhält sich die Destruktion nicht zur Vergangenheit, ihre Kritik trifft das 'Heute' und die herrschende Behandlungsart der Geschichte der Ontologie, mag sie doxographisch, geistesgeschichtlich oder problem-geschichtlich angelegt sein. Die

This unity of inspiration is a point to which we will constantly refer in this study of metaphysics. It is necessary to do so because we want to confront contemporary phenomenology with traditional metaphysics. The inspiration of metaphysical thinking has assumed many forms in the course of history, but nevertheless in all these forms there always was question of "metaphysics." For this reason it is possible to attempt a confrontation between traditional metaphysics and phenomenology. Such a confrontation would be entirely meaningless if the term "metaphysics" could be used for any way of thinking whatsoever. One who wants to reflect upon the future of metaphysics must reflect also upon its past because, if there exists no continuity of the past and the future, there is no reason to speak of the future of metaphysics.

The very fact that we are interested in confronting metaphysics with phenomenology shows that we attach a special value to traditional metaphysics. We are not ashamed to express our conviction that what the great thinkers of the past have called "metaphysics" is not simply meaningless nonsense. Ideas which in the history of thought have revealed their greatness and which, in a sense, have managed to maintain themselves until the present cannot be discarded by any thinker as valueless debris of the past. If one tries to understand why such ideas have retained some value, one comes to the recognition that the great metaphysicians of the past gave form to an eternally human possibility of thinking, the reality of which is always to some extent unconcealed even from one who does not *ex professo* try to give form to that possibility.

By following the path of the intentionality which is embodied in the use of the term "metaphysics," we ar-

---

Destruktion will aber nicht die Vergangenheit in Nichtigkeit begraben, sie hat *positive* Absicht; ihre negative Funktion bleibt ausdrücklich und indirekt." Heidegger, *Sein und Zeit,* Tübingen, 10th ed., 1963, pp. 22-23.

rive at the essence of man as a thinking be-ing. Precisely, however, because man is man, man's essence is always to some extent unconcealed from man himself.[7] In his self-revelation man becomes manifest to himself as the one who bears witness to the irrefutable fact that "something *is*."[8] Here lie both his greatness and his burden.[9]

The Sciences and Metaphysics

There are many ways in which man uses the simple word "is." Every judgment formulated by the positive sciences contains the copula "is." The pursuit of science also is a mode in which man expresses being, a mode which is unconcealed from man at least to such an extent that he is *able* to pursue the sciences. On the other hand, it is also true that the sciences are in a certain sense forms of "thoughtlessness." They speak the word "is," but do not have to ask themselves what "is" means. The task of asking this question belongs to metaphysics.

The term "metaphysics" is used in the broad sense by all those who realize that, alongside the modes of know-

---

[7] "Wenn die Interpretation des Sinnes von Sein Aufgabe wird, ist das Dasein nicht nur das primär zu befragende Seiende, es ist überdies das Seiende, das sich je schon in seinem Sein zu dem verhält, wonach in dieser Frage gefragt wird. Die Seinsfrage ist dann aber nichts anderes als die Radikalisierung einer zum Dasein selbst gehörigen wesenhaften Seinstendenz, des vorontologischen Seinsverständnisses." Heidegger, *ibid.*, p. 15.

[8] "Der Mensch ist der Empfänger der ältesten Botschaft und der wunderlichsten Offenbarung, - er ist der Hörende eines Rufes, der das Schweigen der Weltnacht bricht und den Sohn der Erde ins Zeugnis der seinsauslegenden Rede hervorruft." E. Fink, *Sein, Wahrheit, Welt, Vor-fragen zum Problem des Phänomen-Begriffs,* Den Haag, 1958, p. 18.

[9] "Menschsein heisst: ein Sagender sein. Der Mensch ist nur deshalb ein Ja-und Neinsager weil er im Grunde seines Wesens ein Sager, *der* Sager ist. Das ist seine Auszeichnung und zugleich seine Not. Sie unterscheidet ihn gegenüber Stein, Pflanze, Tier, aber auch gegenüber den Göttern." Heidegger, *Einführung in die Metaphysik,* pp. 62-63.

ing proper to the positive sciences, there is room for a mode of knowing that cannot be reduced to positive science but which nonetheless leads to necessary and universal insights and therefore must be called "scientific" in an entirely different sense of the term.

It has become almost commonplace to claim that contemporary thinking moves again in the direction of metaphysics. During the nineteenth century positivism managed to oppress authentic metaphysical thinking. Since then, however, man has again realized that the absolutizing of the positive sciences was based on a conviction which is rooted not in these sciences themselves but in a very bad kind of metaphysics. As an absolutized form of positive science, positivism represents an implicit theory concerning knowledge and reality in general. This theory is unable to justify itself as an insight supported by positive science but nevertheless claims to be valid. While rejecting all metaphysics, positivism revealed itself as a form of metaphysics bereft of reflection, to such an extent that it even failed to recognize its own metaphysical nature. Gradually, however, it has become evident to man that, if he is to adhere to a metaphysics anyhow, he had better reflect on what he is doing.

As appears from these paragraphs, in its broad sense, the term "metaphysics" is synonymous with the term "philosophy." Accordingly, the statement that certain representatives of the positive sciences reject metaphysics means that they reject philosophy, and the statement that contemporary thinking has taken again the road to metaphysics means that the inevitability of philosophy has made itself felt again. Alongside the positive sciences of law, there is room also for a metaphysics of law; alongside the positive sciences of nature, there is room for a metaphysics of nature; and the positive sciences of man do not eliminate a metaphysics of man. In a similar way our contemporaries speak of a metaphysics of society, of language, poetry, conscience, values, evil, and many other topics. In all these cases the term "metaphysics" simply means "philosophy."

Metaphysical Thinking as Implication of Scientific Thinking

Strictly speaking, it is not enough to say that "alongside" the positive sciences there is room for metaphysics. "Alongside" can be used only in connection with, on the one hand, a constituted science and, on the other, a constituted metaphysics. But such a way of looking at the relationship between positive science and philosophy does not penetrate into the heart of the matter. As a matter of fact, any science demands that man reflect metaphysically because any science implicitly makes use of certain metaphysics. The simple fact, for example, that physical science formulates certain laws presupposes the conviction that the be-ings of which this science speaks can be approached and expressed through these laws.[10] The physicist presupposes this conviction but does not justify it. He does not develop a metaphysics of natural be-ings *as* natural be-ings, but this metaphysics is "lived" by him in the way in which he pursues physical science. The psychologist and the psychiatrist, likewise, do not develop a metaphysics of man when they speak about man in terms of certain psychological and psychiatric laws. Yet the simple fact that they consider a certain type of law suitable for speaking about man implies a metaphysical view regarding the special be-ing that man is. By follow-

---

[10] "Wissenschaftliche Forschung vollzieht die Hebung und erste Fixierung der Sachgebiete naiv und roh. Die Ausarbeitung des Gebietes in seinen Grundstrukturen ist in gewisser Weise schon geleistet durch die vorwissenschaftliche Erfahrung und Auslegung des Seinsbezirkes, in dem das Sachgebiet selbst begrenzt wird. Die so erwachsenen 'Grundbegriffe' bleiben zunächst die Leitfäden für die erste konkrete Erschliessung des Gebietes." Heidegger, *Sein und Zeit*, p. 9.

7

ing the method of the physical sciences as closely as possible, the psychologists and psychiatrists of the past revealed their implicit metaphysical conviction that man could be conceived as "another natural thing."

The history of the sciences also shows that an implicit metaphysics is present in the pursuit of the sciences. Sometimes the pursuit of a science makes it clear that the time has come for a new approach. This happens when the men of science realize that the way in which they are accustomed to speak about the object of their interest does not permit them to express what they really should express. For example, psychologists[11] and psychiatrists[12] have come to the conclusion that justice is not done to the human aspect of man's behavior if their sciences make use solely of laws conceiving human behavior as the result of unilateral and deterministic causes. This realization made them search for new approaches, they saw that it was necessary to revise the fundamental concepts of their sciences.[13] Whenever that happens, there exists a crisis in the implicit metaphysical views with which a science regards the essence of the specific be-ing studied by it. For this reason we said above that metaphysics does not exist "alongside" the sciences, but in a certain sense must be said to lie "in" them.[14]

This statement must not be misunderstood. We do not

[11] J. Linschoten, *Op weg naar een fenomenologische psychologie,* Utrecht, 1959.

[12] K. Jaspers, *Allgemeine Psychopathologie,* Berlin, 2nd ed., 1920.

[13] "Die eigentliche 'Bewegung' der Wissenschaften spielt sich ab in der mehr oder minder radikalen und ihr selbst durchsichtigen Revision der Grundbegriffe." Heidegger, *Sein und Zeit,* p. 9.

[14] "Entre la connaissance scientifique et le savoir métaphysique, qui la remet toujours en présence de sa tâche, il ne peut y avoir de rivalité. Une science sans philosophie ne saurait pas, à la lettre, de quoi elle parle." Merleau-Ponty, *Sens et Non-sens,* Paris, 1948, p. 195.

at all want to claim that the specific questioning attitude of the existent subject-as-*Cogito* in the pursuit of a specific science is identical with the questioning attitude of the metaphysician. True, the specific questions of the existent subject-as-*Cogito* cannot be isolated from one another within the subject's existence. But this does not mean that these questions cannot be distinguished and should simply be identified. Yet such an identification has sometimes been made in the past and has then inevitably led to the greatest confusion. For example, when the positive sciences successfully extended the realms of their interests, some metaphysicians feared that ultimately nothing would be reserved for metaphysics. An advantage of that fear was that metaphysics saw itself compelled to reflect explicitly upon its own possibilities and aspirations, thereby making it easier to restrict itself to its own boundaries.[15] Yet it remains true that this fear of being left without anything to investigate proceeded really from a surreptitious form of positivism. For only in the supposition that metaphysics and the positive sciences are concerned with the same questions can such a fear be entertained.

The Sciences and the Subject

The positive sciences, we have said, presuppose a metaphysical view regarding the essence of the specific be-ing which they disclose. The presupposition is not the only reason why the pursuit of positive science calls for metaphysical reflection in the broad sense of the term. In the

---

15 "Ces vues ne s'écartent pas de celles de la tradition dans ce qu'elle a d'essentiel et de permanent. Peut-être même ont-elles l'avantage supplémentaire de réconcilier cette tradition avec le mouvement scientifique contemporain, en ôtant toute espèce de sens au problème des rapports de la philosophie et des sciences, tel qu'on le posait naguère en supposant le conflit possible, sinon nécessaire." R. Jolivet, *L'homme métaphysique,* Paris, 1957, pp. 62-63.

pursuit of physical science, for example, not only the physical object is unquestionably a reality, but the same must be said also of the subject who pursues physical science. One for whom the reality of the subject is not an empty word but a serious matter understands that it would be meaningless to try to explain the subject, the creator of physical science, through the same categories as the object of this science. After all, no object of physical science ever creates a physical science.[16] The pursuit of physical science proceeds from the implicit conviction that the subject is such that he is *able* to create a physical science, and this is a conviction which physical science itself cannot justify. Any attempt to speak about the subject of physical science in the same way as one speaks about its objects is simply naive and hypocritical.[17] Physical science presupposes a metaphysics of the subject who creates this science. The sciences are modes-of-being of man, and the sciences themselves do not speak and are unable to speak about these modes of being.[18]

Accordingly, metaphysics, in the broad sense in which it is identified with philosophy itself, is distinct from the sciences for at least two reasons. First, contrary to the sciences, metaphysics endeavors to arrive at an understanding of the more general structures of reality. Every positive science presupposes a measure of understanding

[16] "En effet, le *Sujet* qui construit la *Science* échappe nécessairement à la Science, puisque précisément il la construit et est toujours, comme tel, au-delà, c'est-à-dire transcendant à la Science, même achevée." Jolivet, *ibid.,* p. 66.

[17] "Les vues scientifiques selon lesquelles je suis un moment du monde sont toujours naives et hypocrites, parce qu'elles sous-entendent, sans la mentionner, cette autre vue, celle de la conscience, par laquelle d'abord un monde se dispose autour de moi et commence à exister pour moi." Merleau-Ponty, *Phénoménologie de la perception,* Paris, 14th ed., 1945, p. 111.

[18] "Wissenschaften sind Seinsweisen des Daseins." Heidegger, *Sein und Zeit,* p. 13.

of these structures without, however, thematizing them. Their thematization belongs to metaphysics. Secondly, contrary again to the sciences, metaphysics endeavors to express the reality of the subject who creates and pursues the sciences. In the pursuit of a science the subject "knows" himself at least to some extent, so that he is able to devote himself to science. However, even this limited "knowing" of the subject himself is not explicitly taken up and pursued by the sciences. That task also belongs to metaphysics.

Thus it appears that the pursuit of the positive sciences is in a certain sense a form of "thoughtlessness." The scientist uses the term "is" in every one of his judgments, but he does not inquire into the "being" of the specific object of his specific science or the "being" of the subject who asks the scientific questions and gives the replies. It is the task of the metaphysician to take up the questions which the scientist, as such, has to leave unanswered. This task can never be made superfluous by the progress of the sciences.[19]

Metaphysics in the Strict Sense

The statement that the metaphysician tries to arrive at an understanding of the more general structures of reality attains its full meaning in the mode of questioning and answering which is called metaphysics in the strict sense of the term.

Any human mode of thinking explicitly establishes the thinker in the "wonder of all wonders" that there is something to see and something to say. One who pursues positive science also "whiles" in this wonder,[20] but he does

---

[19] Heidegger, *Einführung in die Metaphysik*, p. 20.

[20] "Der Mensch - ein Seiendes unter anderem - 'treibt Wissenschaft'. In diesem 'Treiben' geschieht nichts Geringeres als der Einbruch eines Seienden, genannt Mensch, in das Ganze des Seienden, so zwar, dass in und durch diesen Einbruch das Seiende in

11

not have the task to wonder about this wonder. He speaks, as we have said, in a certain sense "thoughtlessly."[21] The metaphysician wonders about the possibility to speak and about the being of that which is spoken of.[22] He wonders about himself, for his own existent subjectivity-as-*Cogito* is the wonder through which there is something to see and something to say. The broadly metaphysical fact is the subject-as-*Cogito*.[23] For this reason all forms and phases of metaphysical thinking are *per se* forms and phases of a human metaphysics, since they always presuppose the subject-as-*Cogito* as a metaphysical fact.

For all great metaphysicians of the past, however, metaphysical thinking has always been much more than going beyond the limits of positive science and explicitating the specific modes of being whose metaphysical concept is presupposed by the positive sciences. They looked upon metaphysics as the apex, the ultimate possibility of man's questions and answers, the question of the ultimate meaning of being.[24] They regarded metaphysics as

---

dem, was und wie est ist, aufbricht. Der aufbrechende Einbruch verhilft in seiner Weise dem Seienden allererst zu ihm selbst." Heidegger, *Was ist Metaphysik ?*, Frankfurt a.M., 7th ed., 1955, p. 26.

[21] "Die Wissenschaft denkt nicht. Das ist ein anstössiger Satz." Heidegger, *Was heisst Denken ?* , Tübingen, 1954, p. 4.

[22] "Il y a métaphysique à partir du moment où, cessant de vivre dans l'évidence de l'objet - qu'il s'agisse de l'objet sensoriel ou de l'objet de la science - nous apercevons indissolublement la subjectivité radicale de toute notre expérience et sa valeur de vérité." Merleau-Ponty, *Sens et Non-sens,* pp. 186-187.

[23] Merleau-Ponty, *ibid.,* p. 187.

[24] "La question: 'que sommes-nous finalement ?' est dès lors inséparable de la question de l'être des existants en général. Dans cette expression le mot 'être' signifie précisément *ce qui fait et fonde en fin de compte la diversité des êtres ainsi que l'unité qui les relie entre eux.* La métaphysique n'est rien d'autre que l'effort de la pensée en vue de répondre à cette suprême question. C'est pourquoi de tout temps la métaphysique a été définie comme la recherche de l'être." A. Dondeyne, "Dieu et le matérialisme contem-

the question: What ultimately does it mean when we say of whatever is that it *is*?[25] As a rule, man does not reflect when he pronounces the word "is." It stands to reason for him that be-ing is. Within the unquestioned spontaneousness of life, as lived in myths or within the everydayness of life in a technocratic order,[26] it looks as if man knows what he is saying when he says about something that it *is*. This obviousness, however, is deceptive; it is a form of forgetfulness which eliminates metaphysics. Metaphysical thinking in the strict sense is born as soon as man leaves that sphere of the obviousness of be-ing, as soon as he wonders about be-ing, as soon as he is able to ask himself what it means to affirm that something, no matter what, *is*.[27] Why are there be-ings rather than nothing?

At first, it may seem that metaphysics occupies itself with an empty word when it devotes itself to be-ing. To escape from this "emptiness," let us get away from this word and turn to the particular domains of be-ings.[28] We find tools and vehicles, land, the sea, mountains, rivers and forests. We find trees, birds, insects, the earth, the moon and the planets. Everywhere there are be-ings to our heart's content.[29] But, how do we know that all these

---

porain," *Essai sur Dieu, l'homme et l'univers,* publié sous la direction et avec une introduction de Jacques de Bivort de la Saudée, Paris 1957, p. 17.

[25] "So wird die Frage nach dem 'Sinn des Seins', danach, was damit eigentlich gemeint ist, wenn wir sagen 'es ist etwas', und 'est ist soundso', zur Grundfrage der Metaphysik." Landgrebe, *op. cit.,* p. 78.

[26] Heidegger, *Einführung in die Metaphysik,* pp. 28-29.

[27] Landgrebe, *op. cit.,* pp. 77-78.

[28] "Also weg von dem leeren Schema dieses Wortes 'sein' . . . Weg vom leeren, allgemeinen Wort 'sein' und hin zu den Besonderungen der einzelnen Bereiche des Seienden selbst!" Heidegger, *op. cit.,* p. 58.

[29] Heidegger, *ibid.,* p. 58.

things are "be-ings"? Very simple, of course, for anyone can see for himself that they are be-ings. But in that
case we must know already what "is" and "being" mean.[30]

How can we establish that a presumed be-ing is not unless we can clearly distinguish in advance between be-ing
and nonbe-ing, unless we know beforehand what be-ing
and nonbe-ing mean? And since we do make that distinction, no one can make the claim that be-ing is an
empty word. In a particular case it is possible, of course,
that we doubt whether something is or is not, but this
doubt does not mean that we doubt the difference between
be-ing and nonbe-ing.[31] The word "be-ing," then, is not
empty and indeterminate. Rather the concrete and individual be-ings should be called indeterminate. They reveal themselves in their concreteness and individuality
because they can be compared with other individual and
concrete be-ings. Their determinability is increased by
these possibilities of comparison, but they themselves are
indeterminate in many respects. Be-ing, however, cannot be compared with anything, for other than be-ing
there is only nothing. Be-ing, therefore, is most deter-
minate and the terms "is" and "being" are not empty
words.[32]

---

30 ". . . dann müssen wir doch bei all dem schon wissen, was
das heisst: 'ist' und 'sein'." Heidegger, *ibid.*, p. 59.

31 Heidegger, *ibid.*, p. 59.

32 "Bei aller Verwischung und Vermischung und Allgemeinheit
seiner Bedeutung meinen wir dabei etwas Bestimmtes. Dieses Bes-
timmte ist so bestimmt und einzig in seiner Art, dass wir sogar
sagen müssen: Das Sein . . . ist das Einzigartigste, was es überhaupt gibt. Alles Andere und Sonstige, alles und jegliches Seiende
kann noch, auch wenn es einzig ist, mit anderem verglichen werden. Durch diese Vergleichsmöglichkeiten wächst seine Bes-
timmbarkeit. Es steht auf Grund dieser in einer vielfachen Un-
bestimmtheit. Das Sein dagegen kann mit nichts sonst verglichen
werden. Das Andere zu ihm ist nur das Nichts. Und da gibt es
nichts zu vergleichen. Wenn so das Sein das einzigartigste und

To illustrate the reality of all this and make it even more evident, Heidegger gives an example that is to some extent analogous with what he has in mind in raising the question about be-ing. Like any example that could be cited in this matter, it has to be taken with certain reservations.[33]

Let us substitute the term "tree" for the term "be-ing" and assume that "tree" is an empty word. To avoid its emptiness, we want to turn to the particular species of trees and to the particular specimens of these species. Doing that seems to be very easy, but it is not as simple as all that. If the word "tree" is really empty, how do we know where to look when we want to turn to the individual trees? How does it happen that, instead of turning to trees, we do not end up with motor cars or rabbits? The only reason is that the term "tree" is not really empty but tells us something about the essence "tree," thereby enabling us to identify the individual trees as trees. One who fails to recognize this truth no longer sees the tree for the trees.[34]

In an analogous way it is true that we can turn to particular be-ings because we understand be-ing as be-ing and, on the basis of this understanding, distinguish it from nothing.[35] One who claims that be-ing is an empty word and scraps it from his language does not simply remove one verb but abolishes this language completely. Man would then no longer be what he is, for to be man is to

Bestimmteste darstellt, dann kann auch das Wort 'sein' nicht leer bleiben. Es ist in Wahrheit auch nie leer." Heidegger, *ibid.*, p. 60.

[33] Heidegger, *ibid.*, p. 60.

[34] Heidegger, *ibid.*, p. 61.

[35] "Wenn oben auf die Notwendigkeit aufmerksam gemacht wurde, dass wir im voraus schon wissen müssen, was 'Baum' heisst, um das Besondere der Baumarten und einzelner Bäume als solches suchen und finden zu können, dann gilt dies umso entscheidender vom Sein." Heidegger, *ibid.*, p. 62.

speak.[36] The fact that man names be-ing in his speech is not a fact in the same sense as the fact that he has this or that type of ear lobes. That man understands be-ing and expresses it in his speech is a necessity insofar as man would not exist as man if he were not able to do this.[37]

Metaphysics as Speaking About "Everything"

Metaphysics, in the strict sense, is the attempt to express the meaning of be-ing *as* be-ing. Of the particular and individual be-ings man can say that they "are" only because he understands be-ing *as* be-ing.[38] Be-ing *as* being is the theme pursued by metaphysics in the strict sense. Metaphysics does not aim at "this" or "that" particular be-ing but at that which is the ground on which we can affirm of the particular be-ings that they *are.*[39] The range of this question has its limits only in nothing, in that which simply is not.[40]

It should be evident now in what sense one may and must say that metaphysics in the strict sense speaks of "everything." Metaphysical thinking in the strict sense is the attempt to gather "everything" in a rational grasp. Even metaphysical thinking in the broad sense endeavors to arrive at a certain com-prehending, but this gathering-

---

36 Heidegger, *ibid.,* p. 62.

37 "Dass wir das Sein verstehen, ist nicht nur wirklich, sondern es ist notwendig. Ohne solche Eröffnung des Seins könnten wir überhaupt nicht 'die Menschen' sein." Heidegger, *ibid.,* p. 64.

38 "Das viel berufene besondere Seiende kann sich *als ein solches* uns nur eröffnen, wenn wir und je nach dem wir schon im vorhinein das Sein in *seinem* Wesen verstehen." Heidegger, *ibid.,* p. 65.

39 "Bei der Frage halten wir uns jedes besondere und einzelne Seiende als gerade dieses und jenes völlig fern." Heidegger, *ibid.,* p. 3.

40 "Der Bereich dieser Frage hat seine Grenze nur am schlechthin nicht und nie Seiende, am Nichts. Alles was nicht Nichts ist, fällt in die Frage." Heidegger, *ibid.,* p. 2.

together is limited to arranging specific objects in an orderly fashion into a specific region of be-ing in which these objects harmonize. The metaphysics of things of nature, for example, inquires into the meaning of the thing of nature *as* thing of nature. A specific meaning is made into a figure within an inner horizon by this question, but at the same time an entire region of being is, as it were, cut out from an external horizon of distinct meanings and placed in the foreground of the field of presence of the existent subject-as-*Cogito*. The question concerning the meaning of the thing of nature as thing of nature abstracts from the question whether *this* thing of nature is a blade of grass or a layer of earth; and at the same time it constitutes all things of nature, as harmonizing with one another, through a com-prehending rational grasp into a single region of being, distinct from other regions.

In an analogous way we should understand the statement that metaphysics, in the strict sense, speaks of "everything." At first sight, such a claim may seem fantastic. We should, however, keep in mind the sense in which the question regarding the meaning of the thing of nature *as* thing of nature inquires into all things of nature, for this is not in such a way that this "all" should be understood as the sum total of all individual concrete things of nature. If that analogous comparison is kept in mind, one readily understands also that speaking about "everything" in metaphysics does not mean that the metaphysician lets his gaze wander over plants, planets, stones, machines, rivers, mountains, animals and men to make statements about all these things.[41] Speaking about "everything" is an intelligent way of speaking only when

---

41 "Wir befragen nicht diese und nicht jenes, auch nicht, es der Reihe nach durchgehend, alles Seiende, sondern im vorhinein das ganze Seiende, oder wie wir aus später zu erörternden Gründen sagen: das Seiende im Ganzen als ein Solches." Heidegger, *ibid,* p. 2.

the speaking subject occupies a standpoint which makes a certain com-prehending possible, such a standpoint that his com-prehending grasps everything that is as in harmony with everything that is and excludes only nothing.[42]

Parmenides

Parmenides of Elea is recorded in history as the first man who saw the standpoint from which the philosopher is able to speak of "everything" and who thematized the insights manifesting themselves from this standpoint. In a didactic poem Parmenides describes how a chariot carried him to the ethereal gates at which the paths of the day and the night meet. The maidens accompanying him managed to have the gates opened to him. A goddess then appeared and revealed the truth to him. This truth is composed of a doctrine concerning be-ing and a doctrine concerning appearance.[43]

The truth concerning be-ing is that be-ing is and that outside be-ing nothing is. The idea that nonbe-ing would be is utter nonsense. An immediate consequence of this is that be-ing is "one" and has no coming-into-being. It is "one" because plurality presupposes difference, but difference is excluded here. Be-ings would have to be different either by be-ing or by nonbe-ing. They cannot differ in be-ing, for be-ing is precisely that in which they are in agreement; and they cannot differ by nonbe-ing, for what is not cannot make a difference. Be-ing, likewise, has no coming-into-being. For, whatever comes to be would have to come either from be-ing or from nonbe-ing. But be-ing cannot come from be-ing because it is already be-ing. It cannot come to be from nonbe-ing, for

---

[42] Heidegger, *ibid.,* pp. 2-3.

[43] F. de Raedemaeker, *De philosophie der Voorsokratici,* Antwerpen, 1953, p. 151.

nonbe-ing does not contribute anything to be-ing.[44]

The insight that be-ing is and that nonbe-ing is not could easily be regarded as an unimportant truth. As a matter of fact, however, this insight is the beginning of metaphysical thinking in the strict sense, it is the first time that man exercised his power to speak about "everything." To speak in that way man must not speak about be-ing as a tree, a machine, a plant, a planet or an animal, but as be-ing, as not-nothing. Parmenides himself, as is well known, conceived the be-ing that is one and has not come to be as a material substance, a perfectly round sphere.[45] Later metaphysicians did not follow him in this conception, but they remained faithful to his inspiration. For both Aristotle[46] and Thomas Aquinas[47] metaphysics was thinking about be-ing as be-ing. Their followers still use exactly the same formula.[48] Heidegger also is familiar with it.[49]

---

[44] H. Diels, *Die Fragmente der Vorsokratiker,* 1951, vol. I, pp. 234-239.

[45] H. Diels, *ibid.,* p. 238.

[46] *Metaph.,* III, c. I

[47] "Dicit autem (Philosophus) 'secundum quod est ens', quia scientiae aliae, quae sunt de entibus particularibus, considerant quidem de ente, cum omnia subjecta scientiarum sint entia, non tamen considerant ens secundum quod ens, sed secundum quod est hujusmodi ens, scilicet vel numerus, vel linea, vel ignis, vel aliquid hujusmodi." St. Thomas, *In Methaph.* IV, lect. 1 (Cathala no. 530).

[48] "Metaphysics is in the first place a philosophy of be-ing as be-ing or of being, that is, of the intrinsic act (or according to another interpretation the essence) which constitutes as reality or realizes all 'things' in everything they are." D. De Petter, *Metaphysiek en phaenomenologie. Schets voor de besprekingen op de vergadering van de Vereniging voor Thomistische Wijsbegeerte van 20 November 1960,* p. 3.

[49] We will examine in detail what Heidegger means when he accuses traditional metaphysics of "forgetfulness of being" because it has limited its reflections to questions and considerations of being as be-ing.

Affirmation in Negation

The above-mentioned formula describing the proper character of metaphysics is the one to which especially the scholastic tradition of metaphysical thinking is strongly attached. However, there are also metaphysicians, both inside the scholastic sphere and outside it, who reject that formula and even despise it. Nevertheless, precisely in their negation, they start from the implicit conviction that there exists no other possibility to think radically, to speak about "everything," than to place oneself on the standpoint which Parmenides was first to see and to occupy. Their thinking, therefore, is *de facto* also an explicitation of be-ing *as* be-ing.

Scientism is one of the most striking examples of such a rejection. No other philosophy has greater hatred of metaphysics than has scientism. For an adherent of scientism that which is spoken of by the metaphysicians simply is "nothing." Yet, what can such a view possibly mean save that one can speak of "something" only if there is question of a reality which can be disclosed by the sciences? For the adherent of scientism be-ing is that which can be affirmed by the sciences. If such an affirmation is not possible, then we are dealing with nonbe-ing. The position of scientism implicitly but evidently contains a certain view regarding be-ing as be-ing and as opposed to nothing. For scientistic materialism be-ing as be-ing is the material be-ing, and whatever cannot be expressed in terms of the categories of things simply is nonbe-ing. As anyone should see, such a position is a metaphysical thesis in the strict sense of the term.

Analytic philosophers likewise can reject metaphysics only by implicitly presupposing it. According to Ayer, all propositions of metaphysics are nonsensical because metaphysics wants to describe a reality which lies beyond experience. A proposition which cannot be verified by any experience is not a proposition. The fundamental postulate of metaphysics, "There exists a suprasensible reality," therefore, is not a proposition.[50] Abstracting from what Ayer means by experience and verification, we want to draw attention to the fact that Ayer imposes certain demands to be met if a proposition is to be a real proposition, a proposition concerning reality. If these demands are not satisfied, a sentence may have the external form of a proposition, but it will not be concerned with any reality. It is hardly necessary to add that the typical attitude of the metaphysician manifests itself here in Ayer's ideas. He, too, regards be-ing *as* be-ing and as opposed to nothing.

The rejection of reflection upon be-ing *as* be-ing and as opposed to nothing is possible only by appealing again to metaphysical thinking precisely in the arguments adduced to justify that rejection. One who wants to reject metaphysics must begin by stating what, in his opinion, the metaphysicians are defending. He will say, for instance, with Ayer that the results of that kind of thinking cannot be verified, and will conclude that metaphysical thinking is concerned with nothing. In this way Hume also rejected metaphysics in his time, and the same way is still being followed today.[51]

---

[50] "It is the aim of metaphysics to describe a reality lying beyond experience, and therefore any proposition which would be verified by empirical observation is, ipso facto, not metaphysical. But what no observation could verify is not a proposition. The fundamental postulate of metaphysics 'There is a super-(or hinter-) reality' is itself not a proposition. For there is no observation or series of observations we could conceivably make by which its truth or falsehood would be determined. It may seem to be a proposition, having the sensible form of a proposition. But nothing is asserted by it." A. J. Ayer, "Demonstration of the Impossibility of Metaphysics," *Mind,* vol. XLIII (1934), p. 339.

[51] G. Nuchelmans, "De kritiek op de Metaphysica," *Wijsgerig perspectief op maatschappij en wetenschap,* vol. III (1963), pp. 134-147.

Yet, it is evident that such a procedure implies a meta-physics. The motivation of the rejection tacitly contains the condition on which one is willing to accept something as something, as not-nothing. For, it states that what cannot be verified (in the sense in which this term is understood by the analytic philosophers) is simply nothing. "Something," therefore, is that which can be verified in a certain way; "nothing" is that which cannot be verified in that way. In other words, we have here an implicit doctrine concerning "something" *as* "something," concerning be-ing *as* be-ing, as opposed to nothing. There is question here of that inspiration of thinking which tries to grasp "everything" in a rational way, for its protagonists indicate the condition on which something can be called "something." There is an attempt to think "radically" in the way which is traditionally called "metaphysical." Accordingly, the rejection of metaphysics itself is also a metaphysics. For this reason the most violent opponents of metaphysics still have their appointed place in the ranks of the metaphysicians and figure in surveys of metaphysics with the same right as its most devoted protagonists.[52]

As a matter of fact, any philosophy includes a metaphysical aspect in the above-mentioned sense. For every philosopher makes use of a "primitive fact" as the central reference point which is expected to throw light on the totality of reality and help him to com-prehend that totality.[53] For Descartes that "primitive fact" was "clear

---

[52] F. Sassen, "Wat betekent 'Metaphysica' ? *Wijsgerig perspectief op maatschappij en wetenschap,* vol. III (1963), pp. 106-119.

[53] "It is a characteristic of philosophy that, unlike any particular science, it endeavors to reach the most *universal* (the most encompassing) understanding. It tries to understand, within the context of all contexts, within the horizon of all horizons, the all of being." Dondeyne, "Inleiding tot het denken van E. Levinas." *Tijdschrift voor Philosophie,* vol. XXV (1963), p. 557.

and distinct ideas," and anything that could not be grasped in those ideas simply was not. This fact decided for him about be-ing *as* be-ing. Thomas Aquinas, Marx, and Bergson made use of different "primitive facts," that is, they tried to com-prehend the totality of reality through different unifying principles. They were convinced that the use of their principle would do justice to the totality of reality and would not force them to consider as nonbe-ing something that imposes itself as be-ing. In other words, the use of a "primitive fact" implies a view regarding the universality of be-ing *as* be-ing and as opposed to nothing. What, then, is the sense of rejecting reflection upon be-ing *as* be-ing since this way of thinking has to be re-introduced surreptitiously in its very rejection?

"The Metaphysical" in Man

The metaphysical question, in the strict sense of the term, has not been invented by metaphysics as a system,[54] but lies contained in the existent subject-as-*Cogito*, or rather, it is an aspect of this subject, a mode of being-man.[55] The subject-as-*Cogito* himself is "metaphysical awareness," "metaphysical experience." The existent subject-as-*Cogito* himself is a kind of "knowing" that a plant, a child, a meteor do not belong to reality, to the order of being, *on the basis of* their being-plant, being-

---

[54] "Metaphysik ist nichts, was von Menschen nur 'geschaffen' wird in Systemen und Lehren, sondern das Seinsverständnis, sein Entwurf und seine Verwerfung, geschieht im Dasein als solchem. Die 'Metaphysik' ist das Grundgeschehen beim Einbruch in das Seiende, der mit der faktischen Existenz von so etwas wie Mensch überhaupt geschieht." Heidegger, *Kant und das Problem der Metaphysik*, Frankfurt a.M. 2nd ed., 1961, p. 218.

[55] "Hinsehen auf, Verstehen und Begreifen von, Zugang zu sind konstitutive Verhaltungen des Fragens und so selbst Seinsmodi eines bestimmten Seienden, des Seienden, das wir, die Fragenden, je selbst sind." Heidegger, *Sein und Zeit*, p. 7.

child, being-meteor. The metaphysical awareness, the metaphysical experience, is a certain "knowing" of what it means that everything of which it is said, was said or will be said that it *is* belongs to the order of being. In metaphysics this awareness is critically and systematically taken up, explicitated and developed. Metaphysics, then, is based upon a metaphysical experience, on a certain dimension of the immediate presence of the subject to reality—namely, that dimension in which the subject dwells in the universe, the universality of all be-ings as be-ings. Metaphysics presupposes "the metaphysical" in man.[56] For this reason metaphysics presupposes a philosophical anthropology and a criteriology.

Two Phases of Metaphysics

Metaphysics in the strict sense is a "radical" thinking because it speaks about "everything." Its radical character manifests itself in the traditional formula of the metaphysical question: Why is there something rather than nothing? This question is concerned with the universality of be-ing as be-ing.[57]

Metaphysical thinking asks about the "why" of be-ing as be-ing. The metaphysician wants to find the origin, the ground, the cause of be-ing.[58] Be-ing appears to be such that the metaphysical affirmation of be-ing cannot

---

56 "Wenn die Interpretation des Sinnes von Sein Aufgabe wird ist das Dasein nicht nur das primär zu befragende Seiende, est ist überdies das Seiende, das sich je schon in seinem Sein zu dem verhält, wonach in dieser Frage gefragt wird. Die Seinsfrage ist dann aber nichts anderes als die Radikalisierung einer zum Dasein selbst gehörigen wesenhaften Seinstendenz, des vorontologischen Seinsverständnisses." Heidegger, *ibid.*, p. 15.

57 Heidegger, *Einführung in die Metaphysik,* p. 13.

58 We abstract here from the fact that, for Heidegger, precisely this way of understanding the "why" of be-ing is the reason why traditional metaphysics lives in forgetfulness of being. This point will be considered extensively later.

be maintained, be-ing cannot be recognized and affirmed as be-ing, if the metaphysician limits himself to simply affirming be-ing. This realization, which is found in all great metaphysicians throughout history, leads to a second phase of metaphysical thinking, a phase in which metaphysics becomes radical in a way that seeks the depth rather than the width of be-ing. The realization that the affirmation of be-ing cannot be maintained because be-ing does not contain within itself the ground of its being has driven all great metaphysicians to search for something which can serve as the ground of all beings, without itself needing such a ground, and which therefore can explain everything.[59] This all-explaining principle has always been called "the Absolute," in the strictest sense of the term.[60]

2. *The Absolute*

Metaphysics as Theory of the Absolute

Not much is gained as yet by establishing that in its second phase metaphysics speaks about the Absolute. For in the many forms of metaphysical thought recorded by history the Absolute is spoken of in so many different ways that today it is not even possible simply to reject "the" Absolute. To know what this rejection implies one

---

[59] "Ce fondement ultime unique est l'impossibilité pour les êtres du monde de notre expérience et non moins pour l'être humain lui-même de justifier en raison et de fonder leur être qui cependant les constitue en tout ce qu'ils sont. C'est la gratuité radicale des êtres de ce monde en tant qu'êtres. Et c'est l'évidence de cette gratuité qui nous fait poser la question inéluctable: pourquoi y a-t-il quelque chose et non pas plutôt rien ?" D. De Petter, "Le caractère métaphysique de la preuve de l'existence de Dieu et la pensée contemporaine," *L'existence de Dieu,* Casterman, 1961, p. 167.

[60] "Metaphysik hat zum höchsten Thema das dem Menschen übermächtige Absolute und seine Erkenntnis, die dem Menschen Halt und Bindung bedeutet." Landgrebe, *Der Weg der Phänomenologie,* p. 100.

has to investigate the shades of meaning and differentiations introduced by those who accept the Absolute. The Absolute is known by many names within the one constantly recurring inspiration of metaphysical thinking, that is, within the search for that which, without itself needing any explanatory ground, can be the ground of everything and explain everything. Some identify the Absolute in the strict sense with God, other with Eternal Matter, others again with the Absolute Ego, the Absolute Spirit, the Proletariat, the Eternal Return, or Contingency. No matter, however, what the Absolute is called, metaphysical thinking always wants to search for an ultimate groundless ground. When it happens, then, that "the" Absolute is rejected by a philosopher who himself thinks "radically," it is not very difficult to show that he really rejects only a particular conception of the Absolute and that he himself also seeks an all-explaining ground which itself needs no explanation. Marx, for example, rejected everything that was called Absolute, but in his own philosophy the Proletariat functions as the all-explaining ground which itself needs no explanation. Marx's thinking also was an attempt to reach the Absolute in the strictest sense of the term. It is not surprising, therefore, that according to Dondeyne, any philosophy which thinks really in a radical way searches for the Absolute.[61]

---

[61] "Qu'on ne peut remonter à l'infini dans l'explication du monde (*non est procedere in infinitum*), qu'il y a donc quelque part un Premier absolument premier, un *Prius simpliciter* (Saint Thomas), un 'Inconditionné suprême' (Kant), un 'Englobant dernier' (Jaspers), un Principe concret d'Unité qui fonde la parenté ontologique des étants, leur permettant de s'organiser en univers et de constituer un collège des ego's, bref qu'il y a quelque part un Absolu 'qui se justifie soi-même et justifie tout le reste' (Brunschvicq), c'est là un lieu commun en philosophie, le postulat fondamental sans laquelle la philosophie comme interrogation portant sur l'être-dans-son-ensemble ne pourrait même pas surgir." Dondeyne, "L'athéisme contemporain et le problème des attributs de Dieu," *Foi et Réflexion philosophique*, Louvain, 1961, pp. 78-79.

The Absolute Identified with God

A survey of the history of metaphysics shows that two radically different trends must be distinguished in man's conceptions of the Absolute. One trend identifies the Absolute with God. This trend can be understood as a specific way of thinking about the Absolute, that is, as distinct from the second trend, only if one realizes what it means that its adherents call the Absolute "Transcendent," in the sense which they attach to this term. By calling the Absolute or God "Transcendent," traditional scholastic metaphysics wants to express that the Absolute cannot be said to "be" in the same sense in which this term is used for any non-transcendent reality. Man says that a chair "is," that a state "is," that certain ethical imperatives "are" objective, that a child "is," and that a geological layer "is." Metaphysically expressed, be-ing "is." In all these cases man knows what he says because of the presence and the appearance of what he affirms. His affirmation "it is" attains the affirmed reality; man "sees" what he affirms because he is present to it.

Metaphysical thinking according to the scholastic tradition says that be-ing reveals itself as not having a ground in itself, so that man is compelled to "affirm" Transcendent Being. His "realization" that Being is Transcendent implies that he is aware of the "ontological difference"[62] between be-ing and the Transcendent Being. There is a radical distinction between be-ing and the Transcendent Being, so that it is impossible to conceive the Transcendent Being as the ultimate and supreme member of a series. The transcendency of the Transcend-

---

[62] This term is borrowed from Heidegger, but we realize that we are not taking it in the same sense. Heidegger's being is certainly not what Christian metaphysics call the "Transcendent Being." " 'Being' is not God and not a ground of the world." Heidegger, *Ueber den Humanismus*, Frankfurt a.M., n.d. p. 19.

ent Being means that this Being stands outside and above the series of be-ings. Differently expressed, be-ings depend upon the Transcendent Being not in a horizontal but in a vertical line.[63]

This is the reason why within the scholastic tradition of metaphysical thinking one cannot affirm that the Absolute Transcendent Being "is." One who "affirms" that God "is" without realizing that what he is saying does not mean the same as when he affirms "is" of be-ings, has already lowered the Absolute Transcendent Being and made it a mere be-ing. According to the scholastic tradition of metaphysical thinking, the "affirmation" of the Absolute Transcendent Being does not attain "that which it affirms" in the way the affirmation of be-ing attains the affirmed be-ing and makes man "see" what he affirms. All terms used by man to say anything about God function only as pointers, as road signs, which likewise do not go to the place to which they point. God, then, does not appear in the way in which be-ings appear, and the metaphysical "affirmation" of God is not a "seeing" of God.

Our own personal opinion is that the above-described way of metaphysical thinking is valid.[64] We know, of course, that even some theists object to the identification of God with the Absolute Transcendent Being as Origin, Ground and Cause of everything. According to Henri Bergson, the metaphysician's speaking about God pays so little attention to the God of whom most people think that no one would recognize Him if He were to descend to

---

[63] "La dépendance métaphysique est au contraire une dépendence verticale à l'égard d'un Etre transcendant à tout l'ordre intra-mondain." De Petter, *loc. cit.* (footnote 59), p. 169.

[64] Luijpen, *Phenomenology and Atheism,* Pittsburgh, 1965, pp. 64-80.

the realm of experience.[65] For Gabriel Marcel the identification of God with the Absolute "Cause" amounts to a misappreciation of God and levelling of Him to the low level of the unilateral, deterministic causes known by the sciences.[66] This levelling, he says, can be prevented only by completely rejecting the use of the term "cause," in any sense whatsoever, with respect to God.[67] Marcel even thinks that Nietzsche was right when he rejected God because, for Nietzsche, God was merely a God-Cause who was not essentially different from the causes spoken of by the sciences. He accuses the Aristotelian-Thomistic trend of metaphysical thinking of being guilty of such a levelling approach to God.[68] A similar view is held by Heidegger.[69]

It is not our intention to enter into details regarding these objections here, for they will occupy us later. At

---

[65] "Ill s'agit si peu du Dieu auquel pensent la plupart des hommes que si, par miracle, et contre l'avis des philosophes, Dieu ainsi défini descendait dans le champ de l'expérience, personne ne le reconnaîtrait. Statique ou dynamique, en effet, la religion le tient avant tout pour un Etre qui peut entrer en rapport avec nous: or c'est précisément de quoi est incapable le Dieu d'Aristote, adopté avec quelques modifications par la plupart de ses successeurs." H. Bergson, *Les deux Sources de la Morale et de la Religion,* Genève, p. 231.

[66] "Il est à craindre en effet que l'idée de causalité, quelque effort qu'aient tenté les philosophes modernes pour la spiritualiser, pour la délier, pour la détacher de ses ancres primitives, est inséparable de l'existence d'un être pourvu de pouvoirs instrumentaux: elle est en somme bio-téléologique." G. Marcel, *L'homme problématique,* Paris, 1955, p. 64.

[67] "Pour aller tout de suite à ce qui me paraît être l'essentiel, il me semble qu'il faudrait en finir avec l'idée d'un Dieu Cause, d'un Dieu concentrant en soi toute causalité, ou encore, en un langage plus rigoureux, avec l'usage théologique de la notion de causalité." Marcel, *ibid.,* pp. 62-63.

[68] Marcel, *ibid.,* p. 63.

[69] Heidegger, *Identität und Differenz,* Pfullingen, 1957, pp. 70, 71.

present we merely want to record the various conceptions of the Absolute. It is beyond any possible doubt that the scholastic tradition of metaphysical thinking, as a matter of principle, conceives the Absolute, God, as the Transcendent Absolute. This claim does not mean that all those who admit this fundamental inspiration of scholastic metaphysics have also *de facto* always kept this principle in mind, that their thinking has never degenerated.[70] However, any such degeneration has always been rejected, precisely because scholastic thinkers again and again realized that the Absolute had to be "conceived" as Transcendent. In this respect the metaphysics of the scholastic tradition differs radically from other traditional metaphysical systems, in which the Absolute was not ultimately "conceived" as Transcendent but as something "absolutized."

The Absolute as the "Absolutized"

The classical example of absolutizing is provided by the metaphysical inspiration of spiritualistic monism. In opposition to materialism, this monism recognizes the ontological superiority of the subject over the material thing but, at the same time, it exaggerates this superiority to such an extent that the subject ultimately functions as the Absolute.[71] It conceives the relative priority

---

70 "Indem in der Tradition der Metaphysik dieser Unterschied von Sein und Seiendem als ein solcher der Rangordnung gefasst und somit als das Thema der Metaphysik das 'höchste' Sein angegeben wurde, lag darin die Gefahr beschlossen, dass die wesenhaft (ontologische) Differenz von Sein und Seiendem übersehen und die Frage nach dem Sinn der Transzendenz des Seins gegenüber dem Seienden verfehlt wurde." Landgrebe, *op. cit.,* p. 81.

71 "Mais les philosophies idéalistes depuis Kant se sont accordées à montrer que je ne puis sans trahison m'identifier à cette chose, ou même à une chose quelle qu'elle soit. Et sur ce point même une philosophie dont l'orientation est différente doit leur accorder son adhésion. Elle devra seulement se garder de

of subjectivity as a kind of creativity. As a consequence of this, it misappreciates any form of receptivity with respect to that which is not the subject himself, and it reduces the proper meaning of what is not the subject himself to this subject's activity. In this way the subject begins indeed to function as the Absolute. It is excluded, however, that there can be more than one Absolute.[72] Thus spiritualistic monism is forced to sacrifice the autonomy of the "little" subject to an Absolute Subject. The place of the "little" subject who every subject is, is taken by the "great" impersonal Subject, of whom the many subjects are supposed to be merely particularizations, dialectic moments or functions. Fichte's Absolute Ego and Hegel's Absolute Mind are eloquent examples of this kind of monism.

A "Doctrine of God" in Spite of Everything

Like the scholastic inspiration of metaphysics, the metaphysics of the Absolute, conceived as the absolutized subject, also contains a "doctrine of God." For, once a thinker has entered the slippery path of absolutizing the subject, the attributes of this absolutized subject become so fantastic that ultimately they coincide with the traditional attributes of God. An Absolute Subject whose creativity is supposed to constitute the totality of being could not possibly acknowledge a "Divine Absolute," but ultimately coincides entirely with "God."[73] Unlike the scholastic tradition of metaphysics, however, spiritualistic monism

---

l'autre erreur qui est précisément celle à laquelle a succombé en général l'idéalisme, et qui consiste à traiter comme un absolu ce moi dont on a préalablement établi qu'il ne peut être assimilé à une chose et qu'en conséquence il ne peut pas se prêter au type de recherche ou d'enquête qui porte sur les choses." Marcel, *op. cit.*, pp. 64-65.

[72] Merleau-Ponty, *Phénoménologie de la perception*, p. 427.

[73] Merleau-Ponty, *ibid.*, p. 428.

does not conceive the Absolute as the Transcendent, for its Absolute is ultimately no more than the absolutized subject. If, then, it says that the subject knows reality, this statement amounts to saying that "God"-in-the-subject knows reality. And, since "God" is not really distinct from the subject, this statement means at the same time that divine knowledge and human knowledge are not really distinct. The result is that human knowledge is implicitly given the same weight as is ascribed to that of the Absolute.[74] Unsurprisingly, the thinking of spiritualistic monism is strongly colored by pantheism.

Spiritualistic monism, however, is merely one example among many. There are other forms of thinking about the Absolute that consist in absolutizings. All of them conceive the Absolute as that which unqualifiedly is the ground and explanatory principle of everything and itself needs neither ground nor explanation. These Absolutes are called Life, Evolution, Freedom, Progress, the Proletariat, the Eternal Return, Matter. They will always be indicated with a capital because their attributes always coincide with what is traditionally attributed to God, no matter what form is assigned to the Absolute. Haeckel, for example, uses this schema: World=Nature =Substance=Cosmos=Universe=God.[75] Even his materialism then, is a "theodicy," be it a primitive type.[76]

---

[74] "Ce qui revient à dire que la Raison a pris la place de Dieu, comme il est manifesté dans la philosophie de Hegel, ou, plus près de nous, dans celle de Léon Brunschvicq qui affirment la nouvelle dévotion à la raison, caractéristique des temps modernes." G. Gusdorf, *Traité de métaphysique,* Paris, 1956, pp. 103-104.

[75] Ernst Haeckel, *Die Welträtsel,* Leipzig, 10th ed., 1909, p. 242.

[76] ". . . Dann erst wird der herrschende Aberglaube mehr der vernünftigen Naturerkenntnis weichen und der monistischen Ueberzeugung der Einheit von Gott und Welt." Haeckel, *ibid.,* p. 312.

Rejection of the Absolute for the Sake of "the Metaphysical"

In our time there are thinkers who peremptorily reject the Absolute and regard this rejection as the only possibility to save "the metaphysical." Let us see what they mean by this statement.

The best way perhaps to realize what this rejection of the Absolute means is to reflect again upon the conception of the Absolute within spiritualistic monism. This trend of thought absolutizes the "little" subject who every subject is and ultimately merges him with an Absolute Subject. The Absolute Subject is identified with God.

The *reality* of the "little" subject, however, is that it remains a little subject, a subject whose relativity remains unmistakable. Because the Absolute is conceived to think and act in and through this little subject, the claim will be made that it *is* the Absolute who thinks and acts. However, since *in reality* nothing else exists but the "little" subject and since *in reality* only the "little" subject thinks and acts, the claim that the Absolute thinks and acts in and through the "little" subject *de facto* amounts to saying that the thinking and acting of the "little" subject has an Absolute value.[77]

A consequence is that man believes himself authorized to speak with "divine" authority and thinks that his actions bear the seal of a "divine" sanction. He attributes so much value to his conviction and statements that, as

---

[77] "Nevertheless, we must not forget that this absolute self-consciousness is ultimately the consciousness of *no one,* although it comes to itself only through the history of mankind. This implies that there will always be someone, whether an individual or a nation, who will be ready to identify himself with the absolute Ego, to proclaim himself, in a given historical situation, the authentic incarnation, the bearer or the herald of the absolute. It suffices to refer here to Fichte's famous 'Address to the German People'." Dondeyne, "Inleiding tot het denken van E. Levinas," *Tijdschrift voor Philosophie,* vol. XXV (1963), p. 562.

a matter of principle, he is no longer willing to listen to anyone and must regard any contesting of his "truth" as lese-majesty.[78] He imagines that he speaks in the name of the Absolute; he considers his "truth" as God's plan for man and for the world[79] and claims that his actions are the execution of this plan, sanctioned by "God."

Georges Gusdorf

All this is the reason why Gusdorf denies the Absolute.[80] If metaphysics wants to retain its value, it has to reject the Absolute;[81] for, by placing himself on the standpoint of the Absolute, man misappreciates his "personal condition."[82] He forgets that he is only a "little" subject, conditioned by his historicity and his situation. By forgetting this, he no longer remains in the real world and no longer takes real experience into consideration. His obedience to the Absolute is merely a false obedience, for it is no longer obedience to reality. He can adhere to the Absolute only by being disloyal to the human character of man.[83] This disloyalty leads with inevitable fatality to an attempt against humanity. For whoever absolutizes his own subjectivity becomes the victim of a kind of "pathology of truth." As soon as that "pathology" sees a chance to associate itself with the "temporal power,"

---

[78] "Qui se réclame de l'absolu ne voudra écouter personne; il doit se persuader que toute contestation est un crime de lèse-majesté envers l'autorité qui cautionne son attitude." Gusdorf, *op. cit.*, p. 131.

[79] Gusdorf, *ibid.*, p. 107.

[80] Gusdorf, *ibid.*, pp. 102-132.

[81] "Pour demeurer valable, la métaphysique devrait renoncer à l'absolu." Gusdorf, *ibid.*, p. 107.

[82] Gusdorf, *ibid.*, p. 119.

[83] "Le désir d'absolu suppose une infidélité à l'humain." Gusdorf, *ibid.*, p. 122.

the road is free for all those excesses of which history offers so many sad examples. Absolutism leads to fanaticism, and fanaticism needs terror for its own preservation.[84] For this reason Gusdorf is convinced that the rejection of the Absolute, rather than making metaphysics impossible, prevents metaphysics from going in the wrong direction. The elimination of the Absolute makes it impossible for the metaphysician to ascribe any kind of "divine right" to his thinking.[85] Man's thinking becomes again simply the thinking of a man.

An Eloquent Example

There are many ways in which the "little" subject can be identified with the Absolute. Marxism, in the Lenin interpretation, is one of the most eloquent examples. In Marxism, the laboring Proletariat functions as the Absolute. The proletariat guarantees the coming of the universal man. The objective reality of the capitalistic system contains the root of its own perdition, regardless of the capitalists' "intentions." Private property propels itself to its own destruction, solely by virtue of a development that is independent of the capitalist, unknown to him and not willed by him, but conditioned by the nature of private property—viz., the production of a proletarian class. This process is governed by its own objective laws.[86] The objective reality of the proletariat contains the communist future, independently of the proletariat's "intentions." It does not matter what this or that prole-

---

[84] Gusdorf, ibid., p. 130.

[85] "Contrairement à ce qu'on pourrait imaginer, le renoncement à l'absolu ne supprime pas la métaphysique. Bien plutôt, il la fonde en l'empêchant de dévier dès le principe. L'élimination de cette référence enlève seulement au penseur, le pouvoir de droit divin qu'il a d'ordinaire la prétention d'exercer," Gusdorf, ibid., p. 126.

[86] K. Marx-Fr. Engels, Die heilige Familie, Berlin 1953, p. 137.

tarian or even the whole proletariat regards as its purpose. The only thing that matters is what the proletariat *is* and what it is historically compelled to do because of what it *is*. The proletariat's purpose and historical action are visibly and irrevocably predelineated in the entire objective organization of society.[87]

The experience which Lenin had acquired with revolutionary movements convinced him that the future universal man would not be created by the dictatorship of the large majority over a small minority but by that of the small minority over the majority. This small elite is the Communist Party. It represents the proletariat and derives all its rights from them. These rights ultimately go back to the rights of the future universal man, whose coming is guaranteed by the proletariat as it objectively *is*.[88] However, even the Party as Party is obviously unable to think and act. It must, therefore, be represented, and its representative is the Party-Secretary. The latter's thinking and acting guarantees the coming of the universal man. He represents the proletariat, the Absolute; he thinks and acts in the name of the Absolute, so that whoever disagrees with him is automatically wrong.

When matters are represented in such a fashion, it is easy to see why Gusdorf considers it necessary to reject the Absolute.[89] Such a view of the Absolute is merely a sly maneuver to invest a "little" subject with divine authority and for this reason it fails to do justice to the subject as he really is.[90]

---

[87] K. Marx-Fr. Engels, *ibid.*, p. 138.

[88] W. Banning, *Karl Marx*, Utrecht, 1960, pp. 161-167.

[89] Gusdorf, *op. cit.*, p. 132.

[90] "Or l'absolu a précisément pour fonction d'affranchir le penseur de sa condition personnelle; il lui permet de substituer au témoignage individuel un nouveau discours objectif, revêtu d'une autorité souveraine." Gusdorf, *ibid.*, p. 119.

Indiscriminate Rejection

In our discussion of the various opinions concerning the Absolute we have made a sharp distinction between the Transcendent Absolute, as proposed by the scholastic tradition of metaphysical thinking, and any form of an "absolutized" Absolute. In both cases, as we have said, the Absolute is called "God."

The opposition of certain contemporary metaphysicians against the Absolute in the name of metaphysics revealed itself as the refusal to disregard the human character of man's thinking by absolutizing and deifying it. It would be a mistake, however, to think that the Transcendent Absolute is explicitly excluded from their rejection of the Absolute. When, for example, Gusdorf rejects the Absolute, he does not distinguish between the Transcendent God of Christianity, on the one hand, and the Ego, Mind, Life, Evolution, Freedom, Progress, the Proletariat, the Eternal Return or Matter, on the other. In his eyes even the great theological systems of the Middle Ages are attempts to take the place of God, to view reality from the standpoint of God.[91] These systems also disregard the *human* character of man's knowledge. They also lead to terror, as is evident from the procedures followed by the Inquisition.[92] Such a fanaticism can be understood only under the supposition that those who impose their "truth" are indeed convinced that they speak

---

[91] "Le philosophe qui donne la parole à l'absolu a dû d'abord abjurer la condition humaine. Sa doctrine se présente comme le dévoilement du plan de Dieu pour le monde. Telle était l'ambition des grands systèmes théologiques du moyen âge qui dressaient à partir de la Révélation l'inventaire du règne humain." Gusdorf, *ibid.,* p. 107.

[92] "L'absolutisme, pour s'affirmer, recourt nécessairement à la terreur, s'il en a les moyens. La capacité de passion et de haine du théologien, convaincu de détenir le détail même de la pensée divine, trouve son prolongement naturel dans les procédures de l'Inquisition." Gusdorf, *ibid.,* p. 130.

in every detail in the name of God. For Gusdorf that conviction is unmistakably a seizure of God, a false obedience to the Absolute, an inhuman transfiguration of the real man, an enthronement of man in the place of God, a deification of man. The same idea can be found, perhaps even with greater detail, in the writings of Merleau-Ponty.

Maurice Merleau-Ponty

When Merleau-Ponty rejects the Absolute, he has undeniably most of all in mind the God of post-Kantian idealism.[93] He refuses to elevate the relative priority of the "little" subject in such a way that whatever is not this subject loses its consistency and the plurality of "little" subjects becomes impossible.[94] He refuses to let the knowledge of the "little" subjects be absorbed by, and become subordinate to, an "absolute consciousness."[95] He does not want to deify the "little" subject,[96] as would inevitably be done if one absolutizes this subject's priority.[97] He denies that the "little" subject, by identifying himself, his knowledge and his value judgments with the Absolute, can ever derive from the Absolute a guarantee of truth and certainty which could be called absolute.

[93] A. Dondeyne, "Beschouwingen bij het atheistisch existentialisme," *Tijdschrift voor Pholosophie*, vol. XIII (1951), pp. 1-41.

[94] "Mais comment y aurait-il plusieurs absolus ? Comment d'abord pourrais-je jamais reconnaître d'autres Moi ?" Merleau-Ponty, *Phénoménologie de la perception*, p. 427.

[95] "Nous avons refusé . . . de subordonner toute expérience à une conscience absolue de cette expérience." *Ibid.*, p. 338.

[96] "La pluralité des consciences est impossible si j'ai conscience absolue de moi-même. Derrière l'absolu de ma pensée, il est même impossible de deviner un absolu divin . . . C'est finalement avec Dieu que le *Cogito* me fait coincider." *Ibid.*, p. 428.

[97] "Il faut donc dire sans aucune restriction que mon esprit est Dieu. On ne voit pas comment M. Lachièze-Rey, par exemple, pourrait éviter cette conséquence." *Ibid.*, p. 427.

The subject is and remains a "little" subject. Regardless of whether or not there exists an Absolute Subject, an "absolute thought,"[98] an "absolute certainty,"[99] I have only *my* views and opinions at my disposal[100] and I cannot attribute to them the weight of the Absolute. If I do this anyhow, I disregard the human character of man and lapse into "fixism," dogmatism and intolerance.[101] When disasters follow from such an attitude, as will inevitably happen, those who assume it have a "respectable alibi."[102] "Metaphysical consciousness dies when it comes into contact with the Absolute."[103] It can be saved only by rejecting all "absolute knowledge."[104]

These quotations show that the Absolute rejected by Merleau-Ponty must be understood primarily as the God of post-Kantian idealism. It is primarily what we have called the "absolutized." Merleau-Ponty himself eloquently calls this Absolute which he detests so much the "frozen absolute."[105] However, he does not distinguish the Transcendent Absolute of Christian metaphysics from this "frozen absolute" in order to retain it. Merleau-Ponty rejects also the God of Christianity or rather what he regards as the Christian God. This God also asphyxiates metaphysical consciousness.[106]

---

[98] *Sens et Non-sens,* p. 189.

[99] *Ibid.,* p. 190.

[100] "Je ne dispose pour juger que d'opinions miennes." *Ibid.,* p. 189.

[101] *Ibid.,* p. 190.

[102] *Eloge de la philosophie,* p. 66.

[103] *Sens et Non-sens,* p. 191.

[104] ". . . il sait seulement qu'il n'y a pas de savoir absolu et que c'est par cette lacune que nous sommes ouverts à la vérité." *Eloge de la philosophie,* p. 55.

[105] "Absolu figé." *Ibid.,* p. 49.

[106] For a more detailed discussion of this matter, see Luijpen. *Phenomenology and Atheism,* p. 172 ff.

Authentic Philosophizing

For Merleau-Ponty, to philosophize authentically is to seek with the conviction that there is something to see and something to say.[107] But why is there something to see and something to say? The fact that there is something to see and to say presupposes the wonder of the emergence of subjectivity. There is something to see and to say because, by virtue of this emergence, there is meaning, which assumes the forms of truth and value. To speak with Heidegger, there is something to see and to say because of the wonder of all wonders: "be-ing is."[108] This "wonder of all wonders" points to man as subject. There is meaning, in the form of truth and value, within the dialogue of subject and world. There is no meaning in a "world-in-itself" separated from the subject or in the "for-itself" of a consciousness separated from the world. There is meaning in a "world-for-us," which is constituted as a human world in a common history of human subjects.[109] Within the dialogue of subject and world truth and value are irrefutable, and within this dialogue there is truth and falsity, good and evil. But the term "is" has meaning precisely because, and to the extent that, the subject does not seek an absolute "in-itself" or an absolute "for-itself."[110] If anyone seeks these anyhow, he has already killed in advance the real life of truth and value.[111]

---

[107] *Eloge de la philosophie,* p. 57.

[108] Heidegger, *Was ist Metaphysik ?*, pp. 46-47

[109] *Phénoménologie de la perception,* pp. 74-77; *Sens et Non-sens,* p. 187.

[110] ". . . il ya de l'irrécusable dans la connaissance et dans l'action, du vrai et du faux, du bien et du mal, justement parce que je ne prétends pas y trouver l'évidence absolue." *Sens et Non-sens,* p. 191.

[111] *Ibid.,* p. 191.

How is the miracle of the emergence of subjectivity to be explained? This wonder makes it possible to think authentically and to act authentically, but must not this wonder itself be explained? According to Merleau-Ponty, it is meaningless to ask such a question and folly to answer it. Explanations are given in the sciences.[112] To explain means to reduce a be-ing to its antecedents, that is, to the forces and processes which have caused it. Explanations are called for in the realm of things of nature, the realm of action and reaction, the realm governed by determinism. The being of a thing of nature is a being-necessitated by processes and forces and for this reason explanations are possible. But it is evident that man as subject resists all explanations. For whatever would be adduced as an explanation is always a certain meaning, and any meaning necessarily *presupposes* the subject who man is. Consequently, the subject himself can never be explained. Man's being a subject is not a being-necessitated by processes and forces, but a being-contingent, a being-free.[113]

Merleau-Ponty knows, of course, that all kinds of sciences have tried to explain man, to consider man, too, as a moment, an aspect, a particle of the world of natural things.[114] All those explanations, however, he says, are naive and hypocritical, for they all presuppose the being-

---

112 "J'ai pris le mot explication dans son sens courant dans la langue philosophique allemande, qui oppose *erklären* et *verstehen.*" Merleau-Ponty, *"L'homme et l'adversité,"* and *"Deuxième entretien privé,"* La connaissance de l'homme au XXᵉ siècle, Rencontres internationales de Genève, 1952, p. 246.

113 "Tout est contingence dans l'homme en ce sens que cette manière humaine d'exister n'est pas garantie à tout enfant humain par quelque essence qu'il aurait reçue à sa naissance et qu'elle doit constamment se refaire en lui à travers les hasards du corps objectif. L'homme est une idée historique et non pas un espèce naturelle." Merleau-Ponty, *Phénoménologie de la perception*, p. 199.

114 *Ibid.,* p. II.

in-the-world of the subject-as-*Cogito*. They presuppose it without mentioning it. Yet it is evident that precisely through the "existence" of the subject a world of meaning, including scientific meaning, gathers around the subject and begins to be for him.[115] How, then, would it be possible to explain through any meaning whatsoever that which is presupposed by and in every meaning?

Here we encounter the positive value of philosophy in the sense in which Merleau-Ponty understands philosophy. He does not say that there is no God, but affirms the contingent freedom of the subject-in-the-world.[116] Through his contingency man transcends the processlike necessity governing the realm of natural things, and this is what makes *human* life possible. This contingency gives birth to the life of truth and value, to human life as history. History, therefore, should not be conceived as a thing-like process. Man makes history not in the way a force sets a process into motion but as subject, as contingent, as the free co-source of meaning. For this reason nothing is guaranteed to man. He cannot base his hope upon any destiny, not even on any good fortune, but only on the "contingency of our history."[117] Progress does not occur of necessity. It is not even impossible that mankind will fail midway "like a sentence that remains unfinished."[118] For man is not a "strength" but a "weakness" in the heart of thinglike nature; he is not a cosmological factor, but the locus where all cosmological factors change mean-

---

[115] *Ibid.,* p. III.

[116] "S'il fallait, pour finir, donner à nos précédentes remarques une formule philosophique, nous dirions que notre temps a fait et fait, plus peut-être qu'aucun autre, l'expérience de la contingence." Merleau-Ponty, *"L'homme et l'adversité,"* loc. cit. (footnote 112), p. 70.

[117] *Eloge de la philosophie,* p. 61.

[118] Merleau-Ponty, *"L'homme et l'adversité,"* loc. cit. (footnote 112), p. 71.

ing and become history.[119] Man is never "explained," and nothing human is ever "explained" by an appeal to man.

The Basis of Merleau-Ponty's Negation of God

According to Merleau-Ponty, the refusal to explain the subject who is contingent freedom demands the denial of God. Catholic theology is familiar with the idea of contingency. However, that theology first affirms the contingency of man and then proceeds to deduce this contingency from God as the Necessary Being. Such a procedure, he says, means that it abandons the contingency. Theology uses philosophical wonder only to motivate an affirmation which simply puts an end to this wonder.[120] Whoever affirms God as the Necessary Being and conceives this Being as "Cause" of man's contingent being implicitly reduces man's being to be being-necessitated. Thus he ends all wonder, for wonder presupposes precisely the contingency of the subject.

Henri de Lubac has reproached Merleau-Ponty for going so far as to eliminate the problem from which the affirmation of God arises.[121] Merleau-Ponty's reply to this reproach is that he does not eliminate it but makes it more radical, that is, he refuses to accept a solution which stifles it.[122] The contingency of the subject is stifled not only if it is explained in a naturalistic fashion but also

---

[119] Merleau-Ponty *Eloge de la philosophie*, p. 61.

[120] "La théologie ne constate la contingence de l'être humain que pour la dériver d'un Etre nécessaire, c'est-à-dire pour s'en défaire, elle n'use de l'étonnement philosophique que pour motiver une affirmation qui le détermine." *Ibid.*, p. 62.

[121] *Ibid.*, p. 62.

[122] "Ce problème est si peu ignoré du philosophe qu'au contraire il le radicalise, il le met au-dessus des 'solutions' qui l'étouffent." *Ibid.*, p. 62.

43

if it is attached to a Sovereign Cause,[123] as is done by Christian metaphysics.

It did not escape Merleau-Ponty that especially among French Catholics a trend of thinking has developed, compared with which modernism was only a sentimental affair. The truth of such a trend cannot be denied. However, in spite of it, the hierarchy continues to use the most antiquated terms of explanatory theology. This fact shows once again that the recognition of man's contingency as a subject cannot go together with the admission of an "infinite thought, creative of the world." According to Merleau-Ponty, it would be unreasonable to expect that any religion would conceive history as a contingent "melody of meaning." The hierarchy of the Church, of course, does not conceive it in that fashion. It holds on to the categories of explanatory theology, which means a separation between the "heaven of principles" and the "earth of existence," between the history that is already finished in God and the real history of the contingent birth of meaning. Thus philosophical wonder is merely a formality. The resistance which history encounters is called "Satan," but he has already been overcome. "Occult thought scores."[124]

Accordingly, Merleau-Ponty rejects God lest he be obliged to disregard man's authenticity. In his opinion, only the rejection of God can save the authenticity of human history, which has its source in the contingent subject. Precisely because the subject is contingent, the search for truth and the establishment of values, which run their course in history, are never guaranteed.

---

[123] *Ibid.*, p. 63.

[124] Merleau-Ponty, *"L'homme et l'adversité,"* loc. cit. (footnote 112), p. 74.

Christians, Merleau-Ponty thinks, are forced to disregard this absence of guarantee.[125] God is "Truth itself," Truth as perfectly transparent to itself. The Christian believes that he possesses this Truth in faith and thinks that he can look at man, at the world and history in the light of this Truth. He can serenely leave the searching and groping for truth to unbelievers, for he "knows." Hence it is impossible to engage in a genuine dialogue with the Christian.[126]

The same must be said with respect to values. The search for values is of little or no importance to the Christian, for God is "Goodness itself," the Good unqualified. In that case nothing is left to do for man. The laborious creation of a good world becomes an unimportant affair. True, the Incarnation has changed that a little because it made God enter history, but this change is too small to restore "ambiguity" to the deeds and omissions of the Christian. The Christian is not a man among men, because he enjoys a divine guarantee. Unsurprisingly, he falls therefore into "fixism," dogmatism and intolerance. He has a "respectable alibi" in the disasters which he causes in spite of his alleged divine guarantee. Metaphysical consciousness inevitably dies when it comes into contact with the Absolute. For this reason metaphysics demands the rejection of the Absolute.

3. *Does Existential Phenomenology Necessarily Exclude Metaphysics?*

We have quoted the philosophies of Gusdorf and Merleau-Ponty as forms of thinking which reject the Absolute. These two philosophers, however, are not isolated in their

---

[125] Merleau-Ponty, *Sens et Non-sens,* pp. 351-370.

[126] "Comment y aurait-il véritable échange entre celui qui sait et celui qui ne sait pas ?" Merleau-Ponty, *"L'homme et l'adversité,"* loc. cit. (footnote 112), p. 74.

views, for numerous other adherents of existential phenomenology hold the same position.

This fact has led the opponents of existential phenomenology to the reproach that this way of thinking is not a metaphysics. For, existential phenomenology rejects the Absolute in the strictest sense of the term; yet metaphysics reaches its apex precisely in the affirmation of this Absolute. At the same time existential phenomenology bases its rejection on the necessity to safeguard "the metaphysical" in man.

Thus far the reproach is clear. When it says that phenomenology is not a metaphysics, it refers to metaphysics in its second phase, the phase in which man's thinking arrives at the affirmation of an all-explanatory ground that itself does not need any explanation.

Obscure Reproaches

Generally speaking, the opponents of existential phenomenology do not explicitly distinguish between the first and the second phase of metaphysics. They simply and unqualifiedly reproach this phenomenology for not being a metaphysics.

Without further differentiation, however, this reproach is almost meaningless. As we have seen, strictly speaking, it is impossible for a philosophy to reject metaphysics without being itself metaphysics, be it a bad type of metaphysics. But if it is true that a certain form of thinking can reject metaphysics or make it impossible only on the basis of a metaphysical conviction, what possible meaning could be attached to the statement that phenomenology neither is nor can be a metaphysics?

Such a statement becomes meaningful only if one knows the philosophical standpoint occupied by the one who makes the statement. The allegation that phenomenology is not and cannot be a metaphysics simply means that it is not and cannot be in agreement with what its opponents regard as metaphysics. If, however, this is the meaning of their reproach, there is no end to the difficulties that have to be overcome when one wants to understand the opposition of certain metaphysicians to existential phenomenology. What is the philosophical position of these metaphysicians when they reject phenomenology, alleging that it neither is nor can be a metaphysics? What is their metaphysics, which phenomenology supposedly is unable to reach?

The metaphysicians in question belong, roughly speaking, to the trend of thought which may be called "neoscholasticism." However, this characterization does not do much more than "place" these metaphysicians without telling us much about the character of their metaphysical thinking. For, if the phenomenologist wants to conceive neo-scholastic metaphysics as a continuation of certain classical treatises of metaphysics and as fundamentally not different from these specimens of scholastic thought, the representatives of neo-scholastic metaphysics will vigorously object to that identification. They will point out that these so-called classical treatises are heavily infected with the rationalism of Christian von Wolff and they want to have nothing to do with that kind of "paleo-metaphysics." Practically all neo-scholastics assume this attitude.

Hitherto, however, there have been very few initiatives from neo-scholastic circles to transcend this so-called "paleo-metaphysics." Although these initiatives are not entirely lacking,[127] the discussion between metaphysicians and phenomenologists is in a curious situation. Those metaphysicians who *actually* have participated in the dis-

---

[127] See. e.g., L. de Raeymaeker, *The Philosophy of Being,* St. Louis, 1954; J. Peters, *Metaphysics,* Pittsburgh, 1963; F. Van Steenberghen, *Ontology,* New York, 1952; J. Maritain, *A Preface to Metaphysics,* New York, 1940.

cussion and claim that phenomenology neither is nor can be a metaphysics object also when phenomenologists regard these new initiatives of neo-scholastics as specimens of what metaphysics is supposed to be. For, these opponents of phenomenology themselves also reject the results of these new initiatives.

As is well-known, Heidegger has orientated his phenomenology in a direction which he himself calls the "recapture" (*Wiederholung*) of the metaphysical question.[128] One would be mistaken, however, if one were to think that the opponents of phenomenology approve of this orientation of Heidegger's thinking. In their view, Heidegger's "metaphysics" does not satisfy the demands of a "genuine" metaphysics. In other words, they hold fast to the view that, in spite of Heidegger, there exists an opposition between phenomenology and metaphysics, for his metaphysics is not what metaphysics ought to be.[129]

It is beyond the scope of this chapter to raise here the question of the character possessed by Heidegger's metaphysics. This question will be raised later. For the present we merely want to establish the fact that, when phenomenology is accused of not being a metaphysics, the

---

[128] Heidegger, *Einführung in die Metaphysik*, p. 29.

[129] "This turn in Heidegger's ontology can perhaps become important with respect to the question whether or not a metaphysics is possible within the perspective of phenomenology. In our opinion, however, this possibility remains provisionally rather problematic, especially because the sense of what Heidegger calls 'being itself' continues to be shrouded in an impenetrable mist. At any rate, the distance from traditional metaphysics, regardless of how the latter is conceived, still remains just as great. Heidegger is still concerned with the foundation of the appearing of be-ings and not with the ground on which be-ings have autonomy of being. It it possible perhaps to find an approach to an authentic absolute transcendency by way of his first concern? This remains an open question. In this situation it appears, provisionally at least, rather deceptive to refer metaphysics to Heidegger as its only salvation." De Petter, *Metaphysiek en phaenomenologie*, p. 5.

term "metaphysics" is not taken to refer to: 1. the "paleo-metaphysics" of scholasticism; 2. the results of certain neo-scholastic initiatives; 3. Heidegger's metaphysical thinking.

Our provisional conclusion from this fact is that the metaphysics which phenomenology supposedly cannot attain must be understood as it is conceived by those metaphysicians who *actually* take part in the dispute between phenomenology and metaphysics but who themselves have *not* presented us with a metaphysics. It is hardly surprising, then, that the phenomenologist finds it difficult to discover unambiguously what that metaphysics is.

Although it is somewhat disconcerting and perhaps painful to run into this difficulty, it would be wrong to disregard its importance. For, the objection that phenomenology neither is nor can be a metaphysics is thoughtlessly taken over by many who would like to maintain the *status quo* in philosophy. They are satisfied when authoritative voices make that reproach and assume an attitude of distrust toward phenomenology.

In a certain sense the opponents of phenomenology have it easy. They can point out that some phenomenologists themselves explicitly deny the metaphysical character of phenomenology. Merleau-Ponty, for example, says:

What I wanted to say is that the Pope was right in condemning existentialism. A huge number of Christians are interested in existentialism as a method, an entrance and an antechamber. As Catholics, however, they have to regard it only as an antechamber or entrance through which one rejoins ontology in the classical sense of the term. As far as I am concerned, such a procedure is the denial of phenomenology, of philosophy. In my opinion the Pope is fully right in his condemnation of existentialism. However, let us wait and see what happens. As to those who are profoundly interested in phenomenology and existentialism and nonetheless are Catholics, I think that they are inconsistent.[130]

It seems therefore that the metaphysicians who accuse phenomenology of not being metaphysical are right. Of course, the authentic philosopher is not immediately disconcerted by that. To philosophize authentically presupposes that the philosopher establishes himself in the focal point where all meaning appears; it presupposes that he seeks with the conviction that there is something to see and something to say. He starts from a "vision" which he himself as "natural light" is and tries to express the ultimate meaning of reality. He cannot *a priori* say or even suspect what his adventure will lead to. He knows only that he undertakes a task which is imposed upon him by his being-man and by humanity. As "eternally human," this task will never be finished; nevertheless, as long as there are men, this task, together with others, will belong to the authenticity of being-man. Here lies the reason why the authentic thinker pursues his task with such "passion." What is true, is true, regardless of its source and regardless of the end to which it leads. If the truth would lead him to the necessity of rejecting metaphysics, then the authentic philosopher would not hesitate to do so.

Reverence for the Past

This attitude, however, does not give the philosopher the right to lock himself up in an ivory tower. The task which he fulfills has been entrusted to him by mankind, and others have preceded him in its execution. Philosophy is pre-eminently a social undertaking. Authentic, personal philosophizing is made possible by the philosophizing of others. In other words, philosophy has a history,

---

[130] Merleau-Ponty, *"Deuxième entretien privé,"* loc. cit. (footnote 112), p. 246.

and because of history it has a future. This future, however, presupposes that the philosopher takes the past seriously. He must be convinced that the great philosophers of the past have not labored in vain, that those whose system, or rather whose style of thinking, has been preserved by history have really "seen" something. Philosophy will have a future only if today's philosopher does not regard the history of philosophy as the record of all the nonsense which only philosophers would be able to concoct.

These ideas apply also to the special case of metaphysics. Consequently, the contemporary philosopher has every reason to be disturbed if he were to notice that his philosophy does not contain anything at all of the philosophical inspiration which the past called "metaphysical." It is simply to be excluded that any contemporary philosophy could be a strong philosophy if it did not contain anything at all of the inspirations which guided, e.g., Plato, Thomas Aquinas, Descartes, Kant and Marx. If nothing whatsoever of these philosophies is present in a contemporary philosophy, then the one who has authored it implicitly admits that those philosophers did not see any important aspects of reality. Yet, who would dare to make such a statement?

The same point can also be made in a different way. Sometimes a philosophy is accused of having failed, for instance, in completely overcoming Cartesianism. As if Descartes would have to be overcome completely! As if he had simply failed to speak of anything important! Descartes cannot and may not ever be overcome *completely*.

Let us now come to the point we wish to make. It is undeniably true that the history of philosophy preserves a style of thinking which is called "metaphysics." Its inspiration has been indicated in the preceding pages. Since it is a fact that the history of philosophy preserves the metaphysical inspiration of thinking and does not discard it as a useless relic, the phenomenologist has every right to be disturbed when he is told that his thinking neither is nor can be metaphysics. For, what history preserves cannot be altogether worthless.

A Welter of Definitions?

At this stage it may be useful to pay explicit attention to the irrefutable fact that metaphysics is *de facto* defined in innumerable ways. We want to draw attention to this fact in order to throw light on the reproach that phenomenology is not a metaphysics although no one can reject metaphysics or make it impossible without assuming a metaphysical position. Metaphysics is *de facto* defined as:

1. The knowledge of be-ings which lie beyond sense experience (Descartes).

2. The knowledge of what be-ings are in themselves, in opposition to their appearances (Schopenhauer).

3. The knowledge of moral truths, of the "ought," the ideal, considered as an order of reality which is superior to the order of facts and contains the ontological ground of the order of facts (Liard).

4. Knowledge of pure reason (Kant).[131]

5. Absolute knowledge through direct intuition, in opposition to discursive thought (Bergson).

6. Knowledge of that through which whatever is has meaning (Jolivet).

7. The attempt to comprehend from within the "human condition" in its totality (Sartre).

8. Placing oneself, in one's totality, before the totality of the world (De Beauvoir).

9. The stubborn attempt to think clearly and coherently (James).

---

[131] A. Lalande, *Vocabulaire technique et critique de la Philosophie,* Paris, 1951, pp. 611-621.

10. The knowledge of nature, considered as being in a state of rest, immobility, stagnation and immutability (Stalin).[132]

We ourselves have hitherto spoken only about the inspiration of metaphysical thinking and characterized this inspiration as "radical." We have shown that this inspiration cannot be "talked out of existence," so that its rejection is possible only on the basis of an implicit affirmation. The metaphysician endeavors to speak about "everything" by thematizing be-ing precisely as be-ing. The anti-metaphysician does the same, but he reaches the end of his attempt before he even realizes that he has asked and replied to the metaphysical question.

Looking at the list of definitions, one notices that some define metaphysics by describing a specific mode of knowing, while others explicitate the character of a specific object. This point is of importance. A specific mode of knowing and a specific object are evidently correlated notions. If one wants to indicate the specific character of an object, one can describe it as accessible by means of a certain mode of knowing. And a specific mode of knowing can be defined in terms of a specific object. Actually both approaches constitute a dialectic unit, in which the emphasis falls on either the object or on the mode of knowing.

It should be clear now why such an endless variety is possible in defining metaphysics. It is always a question of the view taken of be-ing *as* be-ing. The materialist, for instance, defines be-ing as material be-ing and regards the spiritual be-ing as nothing. The spiritualist defines be-ing as spiritual be-ing and regards the material be-ing as nothing. Both standpoints admit endless variations, but in these variations there is always a view concerning the

---

132 P. Foulquié—R. Saint-Jean, *Dictionnaire de la langue philosophique,* Paris, 1962, p. 439-440.

universality of be-ing. In other words, there is a conception of what metaphysics is, as understood in terms of its object. Metaphysics, however, can also be described on the basis of its own mode of knowing. In that case one will say, for example, that whatever cannot be verified simply is not. Be-ing, therefore, is the verifiable, and metaphysics is defined on the basis of a mode of knowing. Others say that anything of which reason cannot have a "clear and distinct idea" is simply nothing. This position contains a view regarding the universality of being; at the same time, it is a definition of metaphysics, understood from a mode of knowing.

In this way the above-mentioned welter of meanings attached to the term "metaphysics" becomes understandable. In any definition of metaphysics a certain view regarding knowledge in general always and of necessity has its part. According as an author adheres to a certain view concerning knowledge in general, he implicitly imposes certain demands upon metaphysics. On the basis of his view concerning knowledge he can tell others who do not share his theory of knowledge that their philosophy is no metaphysics. What he really wants to say is that, as a consequence of their theory of knowledge, they have faulty views regarding the universality of be-ing. He does not want to say that they do not think radically, that they do not try to speak about "everything," that their philosophy is no metaphysics. And if it happens that nonetheless he makes such statements, the words "no metaphysics" simply mean: "not a metaphysics in the sense of what metaphysics should be on the basis of his theory of knowledge."

Understanding the Dispute

When certain neo-scholastics reproach phenomenology for not being a metaphysics and being unable ever to become a metaphysics, this reproach should be understood in the above-mentioned sense. They do not want to say that phenomenology is no metaphysics in the sense in which even the rejection of metaphysics is a metaphysics. They admit that the phenomenologists also place themselves upon the metaphysical standpoint of the "absolute whole,"[133] that is, they think radically in the way which is characteristic of metaphysics in the first stage of its development.

Nevertheless, according to these critics phenomenology is not a metaphysics in the way in which metaphysics, in their view, ought to be metaphysics. For the traditional scholastic metaphysics is essentially a realistic philosophy, and this characteristic, they claim, is lacking in existential phenomenology.[134]

We see here concretely what we have said above: certain metaphysicians reject a metaphysics as not authentic on the basis of a theory of knowledge. "Traditional metaphysics is a realistic philosophy"; and without realism metaphysics is not what it ought to be. But in phenomenology there is no possibility, so they hold, to speak about "reality" in the "strong" (the realistic) sense of the term.[135]

It should be evident now what the crucial point is in this dispute between phenomenologists and traditional metaphysicians. The point at stake is the "strong" or realistic meaning of the terms "reality" and "be-ing." It depends upon the meaning of these terms whether or not existential phenomenology is a metaphysics as metaphysics ought to be.

---

[133] J. Plat, *Traditionele metafysiek en Fenomenologie,* Nijmegen, 1962, p. 5.

[134] J. Plat, *ibid.,* p. 3; De Petter, *"Een geamendeerde phenomenologie," Tijdschrift voor Philosophie,* vol. XXII (1960), p. 304.

[135] De Petter, *ibid.,* p. 304.

CHAPTER TWO

IMPLICATIONS OF THE PHENOMENOLOGICAL REDUCTION

The difficulties which some adherents of traditional metaphysics have against phenomenology can be understood only in the light of the so-called "phenomenological reduction."

The phenomenological reduction is the revolt against, and the denial of, the "natural attitude." For nineteenth century philosophy the natural attitude was an unquestionable presupposition, which consisted in the conviction that knowledge is nothing but the passive mirroring-in-the-subject of "brute," untouched reality. Moreover, it regarded the system of the sciences as *the* system of "objective" mirrorings. The natural attitude assumes that fundamentally the subject is unrelated to reality and that the latter all by itself is what it is. Only through the intermediacy of cognitive images in the subject is there any contact between the subject and reality. This contact is called "knowledge." This assumption was accepted as unquestionably obvious by nineteenth century philosophy and had penetrated also into the spontaneously held views of that century.

1. Knowledge According to Locke and Descartes
John Locke

Locke's famous distinction between primary and secondary qualities is an unequivocal expression of the same view.[1] By primary qualities of things are meant those qualities that are accessible to several senses. For example, the shape of an apple can be sensed by both sight and touch. Locke's primary qualities correspond to the "common sensibles" of scholastic philosophy.

The secondary qualities, which the scholastics called "proper sensibles," are the proper object of one sense only. For example, the color of an apple is the proper object of sight, its odor that of the olfactory sense. Next, Locke distinguished the ideas in the mind and the qualities in the bodies. Whatever consciousness perceives in itself he called "idea"; and the power which things have to produce ideas he called "quality."[2] According to Locke, the ideas of the primary qualities are objective, but those of the secondary qualities are subjective. Water, for example, having a certain degree of temperature can produce a feeling of heat in one hand and a sensation of cold in the other, but a given shape can never produce in one hand the idea of square and in the other that of round.[3]

At first, this distinction may appear rather innocent, yet it is far from being so. The discrimination between secondary and primary sense qualities contains an implicit theory concerning the nature of human knowledge. For as long as knowledge is conceived as a mode of existing,

---

[1] John Locke, *An Essay Concerning Human Understanding,* II, 8, 9-10.

[2] "Whatsoever the mind perceives in itself, or is the immediate 'object of perception, thought, or understanding, that I call 'idea'; and the power to produce any idea in our mind I call 'quality' of the subject wherein that power is." Locke, *ibid.,* II, 8, 8.

[3] Locke, *ibid.,* II, 8, 21.

that is, as the immediate presence of the knowing subject to a present reality, it is impossible to claim that the primary qualities are objective, while the secondary qualities are not objective. In the knowing subject's immediate presence to an apple both form and odor, color as well as all other present qualities are given as objective. Nevertheless, Locke claims that only the form is objective and not the color or odor. What is behind this claim?

The claim implies that knowledge is not conceived as a subject's immediate presence to a present reality. In that case human knowledge can hardly be considered as anything else but the purely passive mirroring of a world that is "separate" from the knower. The knowing subject is not understood in this view as "existence," but as a passive, worldless subject, and the world is regarded as a collection of "things in themselves," a "world-in-itself," "brute" reality, in other words, as a world in which the knowing subject is not involved, in which he does not live and with which he is not in principle related. In such a theory of knowledge one can admit that only the primary qualities are objective, which then means that only the quantitative aspect is accurately mirrored. The secondary qualities cannot possibly be mirrored accurately[4] because the knower spoils their mirroring through his "subjective additions."[5]

---

[4] "What I have said concerning colours and smells may be understood also of tastes and sounds, and other the like sensible qualities; which, whatever reality we by mistake attribute to them, are in truth nothing in the objects themselves, but powers to produce various sensations in us, and depend on those primary qualities, viz., bulk, figure, texture, and motion of parts, as I have said." Locke, *ibid.*, II, 8, 14.

[5] "From whence I think it is easy to draw this observation, that ideas of primary qualities of bodies are resemblances of them, and their patterns do really exist in the bodies themselves; but the ideas produced in us by those secondary qualities have no resemblance of them at all. There is nothing like our ideas existing in the bodies themselves." Locke, *ibid.*, II, 8, 15.

René Descartes

Descartes' methodic doubt leads to the same theory. By "bracketing," i.e., suspending judgment concerning anything that is in any degree subject to doubt, he isolates the knowing subject completely from the body and the world. Only the subject-as-*Cogito* is undeniable in his eyes. By doubting the reality of the world, however, Descartes did not lose the human world, but simply reduced it to the content of the *Cogito*. The *human* world, the world with which the subject deals, in which he lives, simply became affected with the label: "thought about . . ."[6] For, even if the pen with which I write, the paper I use, the chair on which I sit, and the room in which I live are not real, it remains indisputably true that I have the pen-*idea*, the paper-*idea*, the chair-*idea*, and the room-*idea*. The *Cogito* with its contents is undeniable.

Descartes himself, of course, did not think that these principles sufficed to do full justice to the reality of worldly things. The pen with which I write, the paper I use, the chair on which I sit in the room in which I live are "more" than the pen-idea, the paper-idea, the chair-idea and the room-idea. What, however, could this "more" be? Descartes' conception of the *Cogito* filled with ideas had made it impossible for him to regard the being of all worldly things as a being-for-the-subject. He had already reduced the human aspect of things to the content of the subject. If, however, the being of things is more than being an idea in the subject, this "more" cannot be a human aspect of the things, for Descartes had conceived this human aspect as an idea in the subject. Since the "more" in question cannot be a being-for-the-subject, it has to be "brute" reality, the "inhuman" aspect of reality.

In this way Descartes split the reality of things into a human side, a being-for-us, and an inhuman side, a

---

6 Merleau-Ponty, *Phénoménologie de la perception*, p. III.

being-in-itself. The human side was given a place in the *Cogito*, and the inhuman side was put outside the *Cogito*. The obvious question to arise was, of course, concerned with the agreement between the "inner world" and the "outer world." To what extent does "objective reality" agree with the ideas in the *Cogito*? In this context the term "objective reality" means "brute reality," "inhuman reality." That question was inevitable. Once the subject is separated from the world, the latter can be conceived only as separate from the subject, as a collection of "things in themselves," a "world-in-itself."

Descartes' reply to the question regarding the objectivity of the world is well-known. The world is objective to the extent that the subject-as-*Cogito* has quantitative ideas of this world, for only these ideas about the external world deserve to be called "clear and distinct." In practice, therefore, the world is objective insofar as physical science can speak of it, for only the scientist works with ideas of quantity.

There are, of course, differences between Locke and Descartes. Fundamentally, however, they agree concerning the definition of man's knowledge. Knowledge is the mirroring in a worldless subject of a world that is separate from the subject, and physical science is *the* system of objective mirrorings.

2. *The Phenomenological Reduction*
Phenomenological Claims

These various statements could be regarded as an enumeration of positions that are denied by those who advocate the phenomenological reduction.[7]

First of all, it is nonsense to claim that the objective, real world is identical with the world of the sciences. Even

---

[7] A. De Waelhens, *La philosophie et les expériences naturelles,* La Haye, 1961, pp. 48-58.

the most intelligent men of science would not know what they are speaking about if the sciences ultimately are not supposed to speak about the world in which the sun rises and sets, the world in which there is a difference between being dead and being murdered, a world in which there are lovely girls and handsome young fellows, a world in which I can get to know what the sea, rivers and mountains are by simply going to them during my holidays.[8] The everyday world of life (*Lebenswelt*) is the primordial, real, objective world, and the experience of this world is the primordial experience within which reality, objectivity, imposes itself as undeniable upon the subject.[9]

Secondly, knowledge does not consist in furnishing the interiority of a subject divorced from the world with cognitive images.[10] Knowledge is intentionality,[11] a mode of "existence," the immediate presence of the subject-as-*Cogito* to a present reality. The ultimate decision regarding truth and certainty is made by the presence of reality.[12]

---

[8] "Si éloignée que soit de la perception la physique moderne, celle-ci serait absolument 'en l'air', si, en définitive, elle ne nous expliquait que les pommes tombent des arbres mais n'y remontent jamais, que l'eau des glaciers descend vers la mer sans jamais gravir la pente qui conduit au sommet." De Waelhens, *ibid.*, p. 52.

[9] "Le monde 'vrai' pensé et construit par la science ne peut s'édifier qu'en prenant appui sur le monde du 'sens commun' dont la science feint de contester la réalité." De Waelhens, *ibid.*, p. 51.

[10] "La vérité 'n'habite' pas l'homme intérieur,' ou plutôt il n'y a pas d'homme intérieur, l'homme est au monde, c'est dans le monde qu'il se connaît. Quand je reviens à moi à partir du dogmatisme de sens commun ou du dogmatisme de la science, je retrouve non pas un foyer de vérité intrinsèque, mais un sujet voué au monde." *Phénoménologie de la perception*, p. V.

[11] De Waelhens, *op. cit.*, p. 44.

[12] "Am Prinzip aller Prinzipien: dass jede originär gebende Anschauung eine Rechtsquelle der Erkenntnis sei, dass alles, was sich uns in der 'Intuition' originär, (sozusagen in seiner leibhaften Wirklichkeit) darbietet, einfach hinzunehmen sei, als was es sich

Thirdly, the "brute" inhuman reality proposed by the realism of the "natural attitude" is not the object, the meaning, attained by knowledge. Things are not "things in themselves," and the world is not a world-in-itself. Things and the world are, although not in the same way, reality-appearing-to-the-subject-as-*Cogito*. They are phenomena, but not in the sense of "semblance"[13] or facade behind which a reality-in-itself would be concealed. They are "that which shows itself, the manifest," the appearing be-ing itself.[14] If the existent subject-as-*Cogito* clings inseparably to meaning, meaning likewise clings inseparably to the existent subject—to such an extent that it is even impossible to ask what things and the world would be without man. For a real question is a mode of existing, a mode of clinging to the world. Meaning is the "in itself for us," the autonomy of being with respect to the subject.[15]

Fourthly, the world does not merely have one meaning, the one disclosed by the sciences. The meaning of the world disclosed by the sciences is merely one among many. This meaning clings to the questioning attitude that is specifically proper to the sciences. The everyday world of life, however, is infinitely richer, for the subject is involved in the world through innumerable attitudes, so that innumerably many meanings impose themselves upon him.

Summarizing, we may say that the phenomenological reduction is made by anyone who places himself within the intentional, existential movement which man as a subject himself is, the movement within which things and the world are recognized as complex systems of "nearby"

gibt, aber auch nur in den Schranken, in denen es sich gibt, kann uns keine erdenkliche Theorie irre machen." Husserl, *Ideen*, I, p. 52.

[13] *Sein und Zeit*, p. 222.

[14] *Ibid.*, p. 28.

[15] Merleau-Ponty, *Phénoménologie de la perception*, p. III.

and "distant" meanings, clinging to the actual and non-actual attitudes of the existent subject. To place oneself within the intentional movement of the subject simply means to recognize what man and his knowledge essentially are, viz., a unity of reciprocal implication of subject and meaning.

Misconceptions of Phenomenology

By way of "intermezzo" we may append here the following remarks. From the preceding paragraphs it should be evident that we regard phenomenology as a clearly definable way of philosophizing. We cannot omit protesting here against the many strange conceptions that are current regarding what phenomenology is. Phenomenology is not "a kind of philosophical buzzing around a focal point that refuses to become visible," which is called a "phenomenological description of existence." Phenomenology is not at all an uncritical "slapdash" description of what happens to strike someone's retina, it is not a kind of "philosophical" impressionism. It is likewise not, as Feber naively claims, an "analytic progress of the subject in the direction of the 'things themselves,' which especially in the realm of the physical sciences has produced results that are as surprising as they are imposing and whose far-reaching scope cannot yet even be calculated."[16] Such a statement simply reveals abysmal ignorance of what phenomenology is.

However, even people who can and should know better often make unwarranted statements regarding phenomenology. Jean Daniélou, for example, in his discussions with Merleau-Ponty and especially in connection with the latter's atheism, starts from the assumption that phenomenology may not do anything else but present the most

---

[16] L.J.M. Feber, *Existentialisme en Christendom*, Den Haag, 1962, p. 124.

accurate description possible of man's various concrete situations.[17] He notices that Sartre and Merleau-Ponty *de facto* go beyond this limit and therefore reproaches them for being metaphysical thinkers.[18] Phenomenology, as method, he says, does not permit this.[19] In other words, he assumes that phenomenology may not be more than a method,[20] and when he inevitably observes that it is not merely a method, he concludes that the phenomenologists go beyond their appointed boundaries when they substitute phenomenology for philosophy.[21]

It is hardly surprising that one cuts a poor figure when one enters into a discussion with Merleau-Ponty on the basis of such an assumption.[22] For Merleau-Ponty phenomenology is not merely a method or a suitable introduction to philosophy, but philosophy itself.[23] Phenomenology is indeed a philosophy, the philosophy in which in-

---

[17] J. Daniélou, *Le problème de Dieu et l'existentialisme,* Montréal, 1959, pp. 10-11.

[18] "Mais l'existentialisme de Sartre et de Merleau-Ponty va en fait plus loin. Il prétend ne pas s'en tenir seulement à une description des situations dans lesquelles l'homme se trouve, mais définir les caractères généraux qui sont ceux de l'être et par conséquent constituer une ontologie, une explication totale, et comprenant une nouvelle conception de l'être lui-même." Daniélou, *ibid.,* pp. 10-11.

[19] Daniélou, *ibid.,* p. 13.

[20] Daniélou, *ibid.,* pp. 21, 29.

[21] "La phénoménologie ne saurait jamais se substituer à la philosophie, à la démarche métaphysique. Elle se cantonne en effet à une description des choses; elle ne marque pas les nécessités et les liaisons; elle constitue un complément, un apport, une discipline nouvelle, qui vient enrichir les instruments qui sont ceux de la pensée et de l'intelligence dans sa recherche de la vérité, sans pour autant supprimer d'autres démarches qui gardent leur validité." Daniélou, *ibid.,* p. 34.

[22] Merleau-Ponty, "Deuxième entretien privé," *La connaissance de l'homme au XXe siècle,* Neuchatel, 1952, pp. 245-247.

[23] Merleau-Ponty, "Deuxième entretien privé," *ibid.,* p. 246.

tentionality functions as the "primitive fact" or central reference point.[24] The phenomenological reduction is an integral part of this way of philosophizing. Let us now return to it.

3. *The Phenomenological Reduction in Heidegger*

Martin Heidegger does not use the term "phenomenological reduction." This fact has sometimes led to doubt regarding the fundamental importance of the reduction for phenomenology. *De facto*, however, Heidegger's attacks on nihilism and his intention to overcome the "forgetfulness of being" are attempts to bring man's thinking back to its original source, viz., the unity of reciprocal implication of subject and meaning.

"Explanatory" Thinking and "Existential" Thinking[24a]

A certain type of thinking is current in the sciences. It is the "representative,"[25] the "calculative,"[26] the "ex-

---

[24] Luijpen, *De fenomenologie is een humanisme,* Amsterdam, 2nd ed., 1963.

[24a] Existential thinking is our translation of the German term *das wesentliche Denken.* Transliterated, this would be "essential thinking." The connotations attached to the English term "essential," however, are such that "essential thinking" would convey almost exactly the opposite of what Heidegger means by *wesentliche Denken.* The way in which Heidegger alludes to related terms, such as *wesen* and *an-wesen,* to explain what he means justifies us, we think, in translating *wesentliche Denken* by "existential thinking." This expression does justice to his intention when he speaks of *wesentliche Denken* but cannot allude, as the German does, to *wesen* and *an-wesen.* Despite this handicap, we feel that it is preferable to use "existential" rather than "essential." Heidegger sometimes uses *das eigentliche Denken* (authentic thinking) instead of *das wesentliche Denken.* "Authentic thinking" refers to the same matter as "existential thinking." (Tr.)

[25] Heidegger, *Was ist Metaphysik ?,* Frankfurt a.M., 7th ed., 1955, p. 11.

[26] Heidegger, *Gelassenheit,* Pfullingen, 1959, p. 15.

planatory"[27] type of thinking. Undoubtedly, this form of thinking has a value of its own.[28] Yet it remains true that the sciences are forms of "thoughtlessness."[29] Their inability to think, however, is not a defect but their merit.[30]

What is disastrous in this matter is the fact that gradually many have become convinced that calculative thinking is the only valid form of thinking.[31] Science has made technology possible, and mankind has simply fallen for the fascination of its possibilities. Here lies the nihilism of our era, whose essence consists of the "forgetfulness of being."[32] What is today is characterized by the control exercised by modern technology.[33] Metaphysically speaking, there is no difference between the United States and Russia.[34]

---

[27] Heidegger, *Vorträge und Aufsätze,* Pfullingen, 1954, p. 180.

[28] "Insoweit auf unserem Weg die Wissenschaften zur Sprache kommen müssen, sprechen wir nicht gegen die Wissenschaften, sondern für sie, nämlich für die Klarheit über ihr Wesen. Darin liegt bereits die Ueberzeugung, dass die Wissenschaften in sich etwas positiv Wesentliches sind." Heidegger, *Was heisst Denken?,* p. 49.

[29] Heidegger, *Gelassenheit,* p. 14.

[30] "Dass die Wissenschaft nicht *denken* kann, ist kein Mangel, sondern ein Vorzug." Heidegger, *Vorträge und Aufsätze,* p. 133.

[31] Heidegger, *Gelassenheit,* p. 27.

[32] "Wir bewegen uns mit dem ganzen Bestand noch innerhalb der Zone des Nihilismus, gesetzt freilich, das Wesen des Nihilismus beruhe in der Seinsvergessenheit." Heidegger, *Zur Seinsfrage,* Frankfurt a.M. 1956, p. 40.

[33] Heidegger, *Identität und Differenz,* p. 48.

[34] "Dieses Europa, in heilloser Verblendung immer auf dem Sprunge, sich selbst zu erdolchen, liegt heute in der grossen Zange zwischen Russland auf der einen und Amerika auf der anderen Seite. Russland und Amerika sind beide, metaphysisch gesehen, dasselbe; dieselbe trostlose Raserei der entfesselten Technik und der bodenlosen Organisation des Normalmenschen." Heidegger, *Einführung in die Metaphysik,* p. 28.

Nihilism and its "forgetfulness of being" can be overcome only through a "step back."[35] The return which thinking must make does not consist in a historical regression to the earliest thinking of Western philosophy, but in the attempt to understand the essence of modern technology in terms of the dictatorship which it exercises.[36] As soon as this dictatorship is understood as a dictatorship, its hold will be broken.

The realization, however, that technology exercises a dictatorship demands a return from representative, calculative and explanatory thinking to "existential" (*wesentliche*) thinking,[37] which is authentic thinking.[38] The most alarming aspect of our alarming era is that we do not yet think,[39] that is, not yet authentically. Authentic thinking is the primordial thinking, the dwelling with the meaning which discloses itself as unconcealedness. Such thinking is "existential" thinking because it is concerned with that which presents itself (*west*), which is present (*an-west*),[40] which discloses and reveals itself.[41] For this reason "existential" thinking, as thinking of the present (*Anwesen*),[42]

---

[35] Heidegger, *Identität und Differenz*, p. 48.

[36] "Der Schritt zurück . . . ist . . . der Schritt aus der Technologie und technologische Beschreibung und Deutung des Zeitalters in das zu denkende *Wesen* der modernen Technik." Heidegger, *ibid.*, p. 48.

[37] Heidegger, *Was ist Metaphysik ?*, p. 49.

[38] "Deshalb ist unser Denken noch nicht eigens in sein Element gelangt. Wir denken noch nicht eigentlich." Heidegger, *Vorträge und Aufsätze*, p. 143.

[39] Heidegger, *Was heisst Denken ?*, p. 3.

[40] Heidegger, *Identität und Differenz*, p. 24.

[41] "Dieses Erscheinen des Seins als das Anwesen des Anwesenden . . ." Heidegger, *Vorträge und Aufsätz*, p. 142.

[42] "Sein heisst Anwesen. Dieser leicht hingesagte Grundzug des Seins, das Anwesen, wird nun aber in dem Augenblick geheimnisvoll, da wir erwachen und beachten, wohin dasjenige, was wir

is "thoughtful thinking" (*andenkende Denken*).[43] It is "dwelling in," being present to, familiar with meaning as that which concerns man.[44] The essence of thinking is letting be-ing be (*Gelassenheit*).[45]

"*Dasein*" as Source of Thinking

Accordingly, authentic thinking is thinking proceeding from its original source, the unity of the reciprocal implication of subject and meaning. This unity is man himself, as intentional be-ing, as existence. Man is *Dasein*, says Heidegger, and he defines *Dasein* as dwelling close to meaning,[46] as "existing" in meaning as unconcealedness.[47]

The unity of reciprocal implication of subject and meaning is the "element" in which thinking is "at home" and which the sciences have abandoned. Philosophy also has made that mistake. Philosophy wanted to be a "science," in order to justify itself before the sciences on the basis of its scientific character. Yet can one prove that a fish is fish by showing that it can live also on dry land? Thinking has lost its "element."[48] The result is that man has

Anwesenheit nennen, unser Denken verweist." Heidegger, *ibid,* p. 142.

[43] Heidegger, *Was heisst Denken ?*, p. 158.

[44] Heidegger, *Identität und Differenz,* p. 23.

[45] ". . . wir ahnen das Wesen des Denkens als Gelassenheit." Heidegger, *Gelassenheit,* p. 54.

[46] "Der Mensch ist in seinem seinsgeschichtlichen Wesen das Seiende, dessen Sein als Ek-sistenz darin besteht, dass es in der Nähe des Seins wohnt. Der Mensch ist der Nachbar des Seins." Heidegger, *Ueber den Humanismus,* p. 29.

[47] Heidegger, *ibid.,* p. 16.

[48] "Das Sein als das Element des Denkens ist in der technischen Auslegung des Denkens preisgegeben . . . Man beurteilt das Denken nach einem ihm unangemessenen Mass . . . Schon lange, allzu lange sitzt das Denken auf dem Trockenen." Heidegger, *ibid,* p. 6.

become "homeless." He no longer dwells with the truth because he has let the dictatorship of the sciences and technology impose upon him the system of meanings sanctioned by the sciences, a system in which no one really "dwells." Thinking, therefore, is no longer conceived as the immediate presence of the subject to present reality, but as a mirroring, and the sciences are regarded as the system of objective mirrorings.

The "step back" to "existential" thinking is the phenomenological reduction. Thinking has to return to its "element," which is the unity of the reciprocal implication of subject and meaning.[49] Intentionality is the "listening to meaning" which man himself as a thinking be-ing is. Meaning is not an "in itself," but "belongs to the subject"; it is that which concerns man, that in which and with which man is "at home," that which is "close" to him.[50] When man assumes this attitude, the wealth of reality shines with a new light and he sees much more than he sees in the attitude of the sciences and technology.[51]

Man as "Response" to Being

The wealth of meaning clings to the subject. This statement should not be understood, of course, as if the sub-

---

[49] "Aber das Auszeichnende des Menschen beruht darin, dass er als das denkende Wesen, offen dem Sein, vor dieses gestellt ist, auf das Sein bezogen bleibt und ihm so entspricht. Der Mensch *ist* eigentlich dieser Bezug der Entsprechung, und er ist nur dies . . . Im Menschen waltet ein Gehören zum Sein, welches Gehören auf das Sein hört, weil es diesem übereignet ist. Und das Sein ? Denken wir das Sein nach seinem anfänglichen Sinne als Anwesen. Das Sein west den Menschen weder beiläufig noch ausnahmsweise an. Sein west und währt nur, indem es durch seinen Anspruch den Menschen an-geht. Denn erst der Mensch, offen für das Sein, lässt dieses als Anwesen ankommen." Heidegger, *Identität und Differenz,* pp. 22-23.

[50] Heidegger, *Gelassenheit,* p. 16.

[51] "In dieser Haltung sehen wir die Dinge nicht mehr nur technisch." Heidegger, *Ibid.,* p. 25.

ject "produces" the meaning,[52] for otherwise meaning would be left to the arbitrariness of the subject.[53] Authentic thinking is a "thinking that listens to being."[54] For this reason all arbitrariness is eliminated.[55] Authentic thinking is "obedient to the voice of being."[56] How, indeed, could thinking be called thinking if that which matters to it were not being?[57] Thinking is bound to meaning.[58] Hence man is not the ruler of being but its shepherd,[59] its guardian, in order that the meaning may appear as it is.[60] The being of man as a thinking be-ing is "response" (*Entsprechung*).[61] We cannot understand the subject who man is without the meaning in which the subject dwells, and we cannot understand the meaning without the subject.[62] To think authentically, we must return

---

[52] "Dies besagt keineswegs, das Sein werde erst und nur durch den Menschen gesetzt. Dagegen wird deutlich: Mensch und Sein sind einander übereignet. Sie gehören einander." Heidegger, *Identität und Differenz*, p. 23.

[53] "Aus diesem, dem Sichentbergen, und als dieses spricht sich uns zu, was 'Sein' heisst. Was 'Sein' heisst, können nicht wir, von uns aus, beliebig ausmachen und durch Machtsprüche festsetzen." Heidegger, *Der Satz vom Grund*, Pfullingen, 1957, p. 121.

[54] Heidegger, *Was ist Metaphysik ?*, p. 13.

[55] Heidegger, *Sein und Zeit*, p. 227.

[56] Heidegger, *Was ist Metaphysik ?*, p. 50.

[57] Heidegger, *Ueber den Humanismus*, p. 46.

[58] "Das Denken ist als Denken in die Ankunft des Seins, in das Sein als die Ankunft gebunden." Heidegger, *ibid.*, p. 46.

[59] "Der Mensch ist der Hirt des Seins." Heidegger, *ibid.*, p. 19.

[60] Heidegger, *ibid.*, p. 19.

[61] Heidegger, *Identität und Differenz*, p. 22.

[62] "Wir sagen vom 'Sein selbst' immer *zuwenig*, wenn wir, 'das Sein' sagend, das An-wesen *zum* Menschen*wesen* auslassen und dadurch verkennen, dass dieses Wesen selbst 'das Sein' mitausmacht. Wir sagen auch vom Menschen immer *zuwenig*, wenn wir das 'Sein' (nicht das Menschsein) sagend, den Menschen für sich setzen und das so Gesetzte dann erst noch in eine Beziehung zum 'Sein' bringen." Heidegger, *Zur Seinsfrage*, 6. 27.

to the unity of reciprocal implication. This unity has been lost in the history of thought and, as a result, thinking, man and history have left their "element," they have lost their ground, their source and their home. Genuine thinking is *Dasein* itself in all its richness;[63] it is standing in truth as unconcealedness.[64]

In the natural attitude, which is characteristic of "representative" thinking, meaning is regarded as an "in itself," as a reality divorced from man and consequently as not-known and not-affirmed. Nevertheless, this kind of thinking considered it possible to affirm this "in itself." If, however, one realizes the significance of the phenomenological reduction, one enters into an entirely different dimension of thinking,[65] a dimension in which meaning is recognized as being a human meaning clinging to the subject. Within this new dimension it is evident that without man there is no meaning.

Heidegger has explicitly stated this implication of the phenomenological reduction. "There is being," he says, "only as long as there is *Dasein*."[66] He added at once, however, that this statement should not be understood as if man's existence (in the traditional sense of this term) or man-as-*Cogito* creates meaning. Meaning is not a prod-

---

[63] "Um sowohl den Bezug des Seins zum Wesen des Menschen als auch das Wesensverhältnis des Menschen zur Offenheit ('Da') des Seins als solchen zugleich und in einem Wort zu treffen, wurde für den Wesenbereich, in dem der Mensch als Mensch steht, der Name 'Dasein' gewählt." Heidegger, *Was ist Metaphysik?*, pp. 13-14.

[64] Heidegger, *Ueber den Humanismus,* p. 19.

[65] "Es gibt von den Wissenschaften her zum Denken keine Brücke, sondern nur der Sprung. Wohin er uns bringt, dort ist nicht nur die andere Seite, sondern eine völlig andere Ortschaft." Heidegger, *Vorträge und Aufsätze,* p. 134.

[66] Heidegger, *Ueber den Humanismus,* p. 24; *Sein und Zeit,* p. 212.

uct of man.[67] Nevertheless, it is true that meaning *is* only as long as man exists, for meaning is human meaning and human meaning cannot *be* without man.

Yet, do these ideas give Heidegger the right to say that without man there is no meaning, not merely not for man but not at all? For he says: "If no *Dasein* exists, no world is 'there' either."[68] If Heidegger had admitted that there is meaning without man, he would have denied everything he had previously stated regarding "existential" thinking and its correlate, that which is present. He would have lapsed into the natural attitude of "representative" thinking. Heidegger simply had to state that without man no meaning *is*. One who claims that meaning *is* without man can do so only because he does not *really* make the assumption that no man exists. For the term "is" becomes meaningful only in the affirmation of reality, and the most primordial "affirmation" is the existent subject himself. *Dasein* as 'existential' thinking is equiprimordially speech.[69] "Speech is the home of being,"[70] and being finds expression in thinking.[71]

By way of conclusion we may say that Heidegger's doctrine concerning authentic thinking and "representative" thinking contains the essential characteristics of the phe-

---

[67] "Der Satz bedeutet aber nicht: das Dasein des Menschen im überlieferten Sinne von *existentia,* und neuzeitlich gedacht als die Wirklichkeit des *ego cogito,* sei dasjenige Seiende, wodurch das Sein erst geschaffen werde. Der Satz sagt nicht, das Sein sei ein Produkt des Menschen." Heidegger *Ueber den Humanismus,* p. 24.

[68] Heidegger, *Sein und Zeit,* p. 365.

[69] "Die Sprache ist nicht nur ein Werkzeug, das der Mensch neben vielen anderen auch besitzt, sondren die Sprache gewährt überhaupt erst die Möglichkeit, inmitten der Offenheit von Seiendem zu stehen. Nur wo Sprache, da ist Welt." Heidegger, *Erläuterungen zu Hölderlings Dichtung,* Frankfurt a.M., 2nd ed., 1951, p. 35.

[70] Heidegger, *Ueber den Humanismus,* p. 5.

[71] *Ibid.,* p. 5.

nomenological reduction. His doctrine implies: 1. the denial of the natural attitude, i.e., the denial of the isolated subject; 2. the denial that knowledge is the mirroring of an external world; 3. the denial of the "in itself"; 4. the denial of scientism. Positively, it contains: 1. the affirmation of intentionality, that is, the affirmation of the reciprocal implication of subject and meaning; 2. the affirmation of knowledge as immediate presence to a present reality; 3. the affirmation of reality as "in itself for us"; 4. the affirmation of the existent subject as the most primordial affirmation of being. All these points are characteristic of the phenomenological reduction.

The Problem of Metaphysics

The skepticism of those who adhere to traditional metaphysics regarding the possibility of metaphysics becomes intelligible in the light of this phenomenological reduction and especially in the light of the phenomenological views regarding meaning. Existential phenomenology *de facto* puts great emphasis on the importance of the subject and insists on the human character of meaning to such an extent that it rejects the possibility of a reality-without-man. All this raises the question whether existential phenomenology is not really a form of idealism,[72] and whether the phenomenological consciousness of reality can legitimately be called a consciousness of reality in the "strong," realistic sense of traditional metaphysics.[73]

---

[72] "Kann eine Philosophie, deren A und O das *Ego cogito,* das Bewusstsein in seinen Strukturen und Leistungen ist, zu einer anderen Metaphysik führen als zu einem subjektiven Idealismus, also zur Erneuerung eines der Ismen, an deren Vielfalt und Kampf die Metaphysik und mit ihr die Philosophie im ganzen zugrunde gegangen ist. Wo bleibt für eine solche Philosophie das 'Objekt', das 'Sein an sich,' die Transzendenz ?" Landgrebe, *op cit.,* pp. 75-76.

[73] D. De Petter, "Een geamendeerde phaenomenologie," *Tijdschrift voor Philosophie,* vol. XXII (1960), p. 304.

Regarding metaphysics in its second phase, if phenomenology makes the meaning of reality dependent upon the subject, what would be the use of searching for the Absolute, which, precisely as Absolute, is the all-explanatory ground of everything without itself needing any explanation?[74] Must we not say that in the phenomenological view of the subject this subject himself functions as such an explanatory ground,[75] as the Absolute, and that, consequently, the distinction between be-ing and Being, which traditional metaphysics emphasizes so strongly, disappears into thin air? If the reply to these questions is in the affirmative, phenomenology would still be a form of metaphysical thinking but not the kind of metaphysics which it ought to be.

----

[74] "The roads which lead to the affirmation of God open themselves for us nowhere else than in the world in which we ourselves are together with our fellow-men. And whether or not these roads open themselves to us depends only upon the meaning which one gives to the world, that is, it depends on the question whether the world is seen as an authentic reality, and thus can point also to God, or as a world for and of man that, consequently, can point only to man." De Petter, *ibid.*, pp. 303-304.

[75] "L'affirmation de Dieu deviendrait en quelque sorte superflue si la conscience elle-même pouvait être le fondement des étants." De Petter, "Le caractère métaphysique de la preuve de l'existence de Dieu et la pensée contemporaine," *L'existence de Dieu*, Casterman, 1961, p. 174.

CHAPTER THREE

PHENOMENOLOGY AND METAPHYSICS IN ITS FIRST PHASE

Before considering the crucial question regarding the realism of phenomenology, we want to repeat that in the confrontation of phenomenology and metaphysics the term "metaphysics" is taken to refer to the inspiration of thinking defended by those who *de facto* reproach phenomenology for precluding the possibility of metaphysics. Those metaphysicians belong to the neo-scholastic trend. The fact that we wish to make this confrontation and explicitly defend the claim that phenomenology does not contradict the inspiration of this metaphysical trend of thinking suffices to show that we are interested in traditional metaphysics. We are sincerely convinced that this metaphysical trend contains possibilities which one would seek in vain elsewhere.

As we have already pointed out, those who cannot see any possibility of thinking metaphysically in phenomenology, *de facto* also reject Heidegger's metaphysics.[1] They know, of course, that from the first pages of *Being and Time* Heidegger has always presented his ideas as an attempt to rethink being. However, his metaphysics, too, is not what an authentic metaphysics ought to be according to his critics.

---

[1] De Petter, *Metaphysiek en phaenomenologie,* pp. 4-5.

The fact that their critique of phenomenology coincides with that of Heidegger's metaphysics is not a pure coincidence. For Heidegger's metaphysics is evidently a phenomenological metaphysics, and this is the point that causes trouble. The German philosopher has formulated grave objections against traditional metaphysics and demanded that metaphysics return to its source. A good understanding of what Heidegger means by this "step back" is, we think, the only possible answer to those metaphysicians who claim that phenomenology is not an authentic metaphysics.

1. *Metaphysics in the Works of Heidegger*

In a well-known passage Descartes compares philosophy with a tree, whose roots are metaphysics, whose trunk is physics, and whose branches are the other sciences. Commenting upon this passage, Heidegger remarks that Descartes forgets to mention the soil as the ground of metaphysics.[2] What he wants to say is that, in his eyes, traditional metaphysics has no ground whatsoever. Metaphysics thinks that it speaks about being, but the question about being is forgotten today.[3] Everyone affirms about all kinds of things that they *are*; everyone considers this expression to be intelligible without any further ado.[4] However, this obviousness is dangerous and deceptive, for the meaning of being is not at all intelligible without any further ado. The question about being has to be raised again.[5]

Yet, it is very difficult to raise this question, because traditional metaphysics has blocked the road to a correct

---

[2] Heidegger, *Was ist Metaphysik ?*, p. 7.

[3] "Die genannte Frage ist heute in Vergessenheit gekommen." Heidegger, *Sein und Zeit*, p. 2.

[4] *Ibid.*, p. 4.

[5] *Ibid.*, p. 3.

understanding.[6] For this reason the road to a correct understanding of being has first to be re-opened. This road lies in the analysis of *Dasein*, the being of man, for man is the only be-ing among all be-ings for which, in its being, being itself is an issue.[7] Man asks about being in general, and this question itself is a mode of being of *Dasein*;[8] man's own being is an issue in his being, that is, *Dasein* is characterized by understanding of itself. For this reason man's "self-awareness" contains also a measure of awareness of being in general. Otherwise man would not even be able to ask the question about being.[9]

The "Ontological Difference"

How did it happen that traditional metaphysics blocked the road toward an authentic idea of being? Heidegger addresses to the metaphysics of the past the reproach that it has always reflected upon be-ing as be-ing, rather than on being as being.[10]

We interrupt this explanation of Heidegger's metaphysics to point out that, as soon as Heidegger makes this remark, scholastic metaphysicians reply at once: this critique of traditional metaphysics may be valid for many forms of metaphysics but not for that of Thomas Aquinas.[11] The latter, they say, did reflect upon being (*esse*).

---

[6] *Ibid.*, pp. 19-22.

[7] "Das Dasein . . . ist vielmehr dadurch ontisch ausgezeichnet, dass es diesem Seienden in seinem Sein um dieses Sein selbst geht . . . Seinsverständnis ist selbst eine Seinsbestimmtheit des Daseins." *Ibid.*, p. 12.

[8] *Ibid.*, pp. 7, 12-13, 15.

[9] *Ibid.*, pp. 5-6.

[10] "Weil die Metaphysik das Seiende als das Seiende befragt, bleibt sie beim Seienden und kehrt sich nicht an das Sein als Sein." Heidegger, *Was ist Metaphysik ?*, p. 8.

[11] "Nach dem vorhin über Thomas von Aquin Gesagten blieb wenigstens bei ihm die Frage nach dem Sein nicht ungedacht,

True, he called be-ing (*ens*) the formal object of the intellect, but he also added that be-ing is be-ing only through the act of being (*actus essendi*) or *esse*. In other words, for Thomas Aquinas there can be no question of really understanding be-ing (*ens*) unless one penetrates into the being (*esse*) through which alone be-ing is be-ing. For this reason, they say, St. Thomas' thinking listened to the "call of being"; he was able to rise above the pseudo-thinking which talks learnedly about the concept of be-ing but does not understand the "call of being." It enabled him to go forward to the affirmation of Subsistent Being.[12]

These words are almost a literal quotation of the view held by J. Lotz. However, he is far from being the only one to hold that position. Yet we ask ourselves whether Heidegger's opponents really think that he knows almost nothing about scholastic metaphysics and would regard their reply as a genuine revelation of something he had never suspected. As a matter of fact, Heidegger is fully acquainted with the scholastic distinction between be-ing (*ens*), act of being (*actus essendi* or *esse*), and Subsistent Being. Nevertheless, scholastic metaphysics is included in his complaint that man's thinking has stopped with the reflection upon be-ing as be-ing and forgotten about being. If Heidegger's terms *Seiende* and *Sein* were simply identical with the *ens* and *esse* of Thomas Aquinas, his opponents would be right, of course, in claiming that St. Thomas did not confuse these terms. However, abstracting from the question regarding the value of Heidegger's terminology, we must emphasize that it differs greatly from that of Thomas Aquinas. Thomism is undoubtedly a

weshalb die Metaphysik wenigstens für ihn jene Frage nicht nur mitumfasst, sondern letztlich zum Kern alles Fragens erhebt." J. Lotz, "Denken und Sein nach den jüngsten Veröffentlichungen von M. Heidegger," *Scholastik,* vol. XXXIII (1958), p. 83.

12 Lotz, *ibid.,* p. 81-82.

reply to a question about being, but it does not answer the question raised by Heidegger.

How different Heidegger's question is becomes evident when one realizes why he addresses traditional metaphysics with the reproach of not having arrived at a concept of being as truth and of truth as unconcealedness.[13] According to Heidegger, the truth of being has remained hidden from metaphysics from Anaximander to Nietzsche.[14] The result was that being and be-ing were constantly confused.[15] That confusion should not be regarded as a simple mistake or carelessness, for it is an event affecting the entire history of mankind. Humanity lives in nihilism, and this nihilism is "forgetfulness of being."[16] Mankind disregards the "ontological difference,"[17] the distinction between be-ing and being.

For this reason metaphysics must be transcended. The experience that "being has been forgotten" must lead thinking to become "more thoughtful."[18] It does not become more thoughtful if one simply tries to make a greater effort but only if one replaces the "representation of be-ing" by a reflection in which the truth of being is seen "in relation to man's essence."[19] In saying this, Heideg-

---

[13] "Aber die Metaphysik bringt das Sein selbst nicht zur Sprache, weil sie das Sein nicht in seiner Wahrheit und die Wahrheit nicht als die Unverborgenheit und diese nicht in ihrem Wesen bedenkt." Heidegger, *Was ist Metaphysik?*, p. 10.

[14] Heidegger, *ibid.*, p. 11.

[15] "Das Aussagen der Metaphysik bewegt sich von ihrem Beginn bis in ihre Vollendung auf eine seltsame Weise in einer durchgängigen Verwechslung von Seiendem und Sein." Heidegger, *ibid.*, p. 10.

[16] Heidegger, *Zur Seinsfrage, passim.*

[17] Heidegger, *Identität und Differenz, passim.*

[18] Heidegger, *Was ist Metaphysik ?*, pp. 12-13.

[19] Heidegger, *ibid.*, p. 13; "Das Denken auf einen Weg zu bringen, durch den es in den Bezug der Wahrheit des Seins zum Wesen des Menschen gelangt, damit es das Sein selbst in seiner Wahrheit

ger wants to express that in "representative thinking about be-ing" be-ing is conceived as *not* related to the essence of man. This is the case with the "natural attitude." That this statement contains what Heidegger wants to say is confirmed by his demand that thinking, in order to overcome the "forgetfulness of being," pass from "representative thinking" to "thoughtful thinking."[20] The latter he calls also "existential thinking," which, unlike "representative thinking," is not characterized by the "natural attitude" that claims to have the "in itself" mirrored in its thinking.

Accordingly, the demand that "representative thinking about be-ing" be replaced by "thoughtful thinking about being" means that Heidegger wants us to give up the "natural attitude" and to perform the phenomenological reduction. The be-ing with which metaphysics has always occupied itself is, for Heidegger, the "in itself," "brute" reality, and being is for him identical with what the French phenomenologists call the "in itself for us" (*en-soi-pour-nous*),[21] or meaning.[22] Heidegger's being is truth-as-unconcealedness, meaning as term of encounter.

"Being" and *"No-thingness"*

An analysis of what Heidegger calls "no-thingness" leads to the same conclusion. The sciences, he says, are

eigens bedenke, dahin ist das in 'Sein und Zeit' versuchte Denken unterwegs."

[20] Heidegger, *ibid.,* p. 21.

[21] "Sein ist nicht mit der Beschaffenheit ausgestattet, dass es sich entbirgt, sondern das Sichentbergen gehört zum Eigenen des Seins. Sein hat sein Eigenes im Sichentbergen. Sein ist nicht zuvor etwas für sich, das dann erst ein Sichentbergen bewerkstelligt." Heidegger, *Der Satz vom Grund,* pp. 120-121.

[22] "Die Lichtung ist selbst ein Grundzug des Seins und nicht dessen Folge." Heidegger, *Nietzsche,* Pfullingen, 1961, vol. II, p. **490.**

concerned solely with be-ing and with "nothing" else.[23] From a freely chosen attitude or standpoint they question be-ing; be-ing is their beginning and their end; and precisely in this way man secures mastership over be-ing.[24] The sciences are interested only in be-ing and want to have nothing to do with "no-thingness." Yet, is it possible to persevere in that professed indifference? Is it possible to put the essence of the sciences in words without making an appeal to "no-thingness"? That question must be answered in the negative.[25] Let us see why.

The sciences have as their task to "explain." They tend to reduce cosmic be-ing to its antecedents, to the cosmic processes and forces which make the be-ing be. How, however, is such "explaining" possible? If man himself is also a be-ing like all the other be-ings explained by the sciences, there would be only darkness. The light of scientific explanation would shine nowhere; be-ing would not be "manifest" (*offenbar*) and would not give man something to say and something to think about. But cosmic be-ing *is* "manifest," it does give man something to say and something to think about. The reason is solely that man himself, *Dasein*, is not, strictly speaking, a be-ing. If be-ing is to be able to appear and relate to *Dasein*, then *Dasein* must transcend the aspect of "cosmic be-ing" that is found also in man. For otherwise *Dasein* could not relate to be-ing and to itself,[26] since cosmic be-ings do

---

[23] "Erforscht werden soll nur das Seiende und sonst - nichts; das Seiende allein und weiter - nichts; das Seiende einzig und darüber hinaus - nichts." Heidegger, *Was ist Metaphysik ?*, p. 26.

[24] Heidegger, *ibid.*, p. 25.

[25] "Die Wissenschaft will vom Nichts nichts wissen. Aber ebenso gewiss bleibt bestehen: dort, wo sie ihr eigenes Wesen auszusprechen versucht, ruft sie das Nichts zu Hilfe. Was sie verwirft, nimmt sie in Anspruch." Heidegger, *ibid.*, p. 27.

[26] "Würde das Dasein im Grunde seines Wesens nicht transzendieren . . . dann könnte es sich nie zu Seiendem verhalten, also auch nicht zu sich selbst." Heidegger, *ibid.*, p. 35.

not relate to themselves and to one another.

What is it in *Dasein* that makes it transcend the aspect of "cosmic be-ing" that is in *Dasein* itself? That has to be other-than-be-ing, of course, and the other-than-be-ing is "no-thing." "*Dasein* means being projected into 'no-thingness'."[27] "No-thingness" makes it possible for be-ing to reveal itself and for *Dasein* to be open to itself.[28] "No-thing," then, is not a negative nothing, a simple denial of the concept "be-ing,"[29] for the self-revelation of be-ings occurs through the "nihilation of 'no-thingness'."[30] Hence it is something very positive. In this way it becomes clear that the sciences which are interested in explaining be-ing and in nothing else cannot understand themselves without knowledge of "no-thingness." For it is precisely "being projected into 'no-thingness'" that makes the sciences possible.[31]

Heidegger here conceives man as the oppositional unity of be-ing and "no-thingness." By "be-ing" he means the cosmic be-ing that can be explained by the sciences. A scientific explanation is possible because in *Dasein* man transcends the be-ing which is found also in himself. Heidegger calls the transcending aspect of man "no-thingness" because it cannot be like the be-ing explained by the sciences, since objects of the sciences do not pursue

---

27 Heidegger, *ibid.*, p. 35.

28 "Ohne ursprüngliche Offenbarkeit des Nichts kein Selbstsein und keine Freiheit." Heidegger, *ibid.*, p. 35.

29 "Das Nichts ist die Ermöglichung der Offenbarkeit des Seienden als eines solchen für das menschliche Dasein. Das Nichts gibt nicht erst den Gegenbegriff zum Seienden her, sondern gehört ursprünglich zum Wesen selbst." Heidegger, *ibid.*, p. 35.

30 "Im Sein des Seienden geschieht das Nichten des Nichts." Heidegger, *ibid.*, p. 35.

31 Jetzt aber wird im Fragen nach dem Nichts offenbar, dass dieses wissenschaftliche Dasein nur möglich ist, wenn es sich im Vorhinein in das Nichts hineinhält." Heidegger, *ibid.*, p. 40.

any science. Accordingly, Heidegger's "other than be-ing" clearly is the subject, the existent subject-as-*Cogito*, which makes possible man's wonder, his asking about the "why" of be-ings, his science.[32] Although he calls this subject "no-thing" because it is not what he has called "be-ing," this "no-thing" is something positive. It is the positivity of the existent subject as "letting be." In this way the apparently nonsensical statement: "Every be-ing as be-ing comes to be from no-thing," becomes intelligible.[33] There is meaning because of the "no-thingness" of *Dasein*, that is, because of the positivity of subjectivity, through which man transcends the being of cosmic be-ing in himself.[34]

These explanations refer only to the first phase of Heidegger's reflection upon "no-thingness." "No-thingness" is the subject-as-*Cogito*. Heidegger, however, reflects upon "no-thing" in two phases. He speaks about "no-thingness" not only in reference to *Dasein's* transcendence of the aspect of "cosmic be-ing" in itself, the transcendence of the subject, but also calls be-ing "no-thing" in reference to *Dasein*. He does this in his reflection upon dread.

----

[32] "Einzig weil das Nichts des Daseins offenbar ist, kann die volle Befremdlichkeit des Seienden über uns kommen. Nur wenn die Befremdlichkeit des Seienden uns bedrängt, weckt es und zieht es sich die Verwunderung. Nur auf dem Grunde der Verwunderung - d.h. der Offenbarkeit des Nichts - entspringt das 'Warum'. Nur weil das Warum als solches möglich ist, können wir in bestimmter Weise nach Gründen fragen und begründen. Nur weil wir fragen und begründen können, ist unserer Existenz das Schicksal des Forschers in die Hand gegeben." Heidegger, *ibid.*, p. 41.

[33] Heidegger, *ibid.*, p. 40.

[34] "Im Nichts des Daseins kommt erst das Seiende im Ganze seiner eigensten Möglichkeit mach, d.h. in endlicher Weise, zu sich selbst." Heidegger, *ibid.*, p. 40.

The experience of "no-thing," he says, is dread.[35] Dread is that event in *Dasein* which reveals "no-thing" and therefore must be the starting point of our questioning.[36] At first, it appears that such a questioning is not possible. We ask: "What is 'no-thing'?" But by asking the question in that way, we question "no-thing" as if it were something, we question it as be-ing. Yet "no-thing" is distinct precisely from be-ing. Put in this way, therefore, the question deprives itself of its object.[37] The sciences are interested in be-ings. One who conceives the question: "What is 'no-thing'?" as a scientific question begins by regarding "no-thing" as something. Since "nothing" is the negation of something, the scientific way of asking the question is left without an object. The sciences are unable to ask the question about "no-thing." This inability is annoying only to those who think that scientific questions and scientific thinking are the only possible modes of asking questions and of thinking. That position, however, is untenable.[38]

We know "no-thing," at least as that which we dismiss in our speaking. In dread, however, "no-thing" reveals itself. In dread *Dasein* finds itself completely powerless because the totality of be-ing slips away. In dread be-ing reveals itself as "no-thing." Man knows this, for, as soon as his dread passes, he can only say: "It was nothing."[39] That which makes man dread is never a particular be-ing. Dread differs from anxiety, which is always directed to a particular be-ing. In dread, however, man faces the

---

[35] Heidegger *ibid.,* p. 32.

[36] "Mit der Grundstimmung der Angst haben wir das Geschehen des Daseins erreicht, in dem das Nichts offenbar ist und aus dem heraus es befragt werden muss." Heidegger, *ibid.,* p. 33.

[37] Heidegger, *ibid.,* p. 27.

[38] Heidegger, *Einführung in die Metaphysik,* p. 20.

[39] Heidegger, *Was ist Metaphysik ?,* p. 32.

totality of be-ing as something against which he is power-less.[40] In dread "no-thing" nihilates be-ing in its totality.

Thus, as we have seen, Heidegger first called the subject, as other-than-be-ing, "no-thing," and now be-ing also reveals itself as "no-thing" in opposition to *Dasein*. Does it not follow that such a philosophy of "no-thingness" is an absolute nihilism? Heidegger himself replies in the negative to this question. For "no-thing" reveals itself in dread as other-than-be-ing, that is, it reveals itself as being.[41] Being does not let itself be "represented" as a be-ing. The other-than-be-ing is the nonbe-ing. Yet this "no-thing" presents itself as being.[42]

The sense of these seemingly enigmatic formulae becomes clear when we recall what Heidegger has in mind in saying that be-ing is "represented" while being is not "represented." "Representative" thought is pursued by the sciences. They claim to mirror the "in itself," "brute" reality, in an exact way. For this reason their thinking is also called "calculative" thinking.[43] As long as one remains within the limits of their claim, *Dasein* feels secure. This security and peace, however, are illusory. They can collapse at any moment. This happens when *Dasein* comes to the realization that be-ing precisely as "in itself" is meaningless. "Represented" as "in itself," be-ing is simply "nothing." All security, peace and cer-

---

[40] "Die Abweisung von sich ist aber als solche das entgleiten-lassende Verweisen auf das versinkende Seiende im Ganze." Heidegger, *ibid.*, p. 34.

[41] "Die rechte Stellungnahme zu diesen Sätzen . . . mag prüfen, ob das Nichts, das die Angst in ihr Wesen stimmt, sich bei einer leeren Verneinung alles Seienden erschöpft, oder ob, was nie und nirgends ein Seiendes ist, sich entschleiert als das von allem Seienden Sichunterscheidende, das wir das Sein nennen." Heidegger, *ibid.*, p. 45.

[42] Heidegger, *ibid.*, p. 45.

[43] Heidegger, *ibid.*, p. 48.

tainty based on the claims of calculative thinking vanish, for " 'nothing' is unqualified concealment."[44] The subject finds himself as dread or, in Merleau-Ponty's words as "dizziness." As dizziness facing meaninglessness or the "nothing" of the "in itself," however, *Dasein* does not face pure nothing, negative nothingness.[45] For "no-thing" presents itself as being, that is, meaning or the "in itself for us" reveals itself as that which offers food for thought to "existential" thinking.[46] The "no-thing" is only the "nothingness" of the "in itself," and the revelation of this "nothingness" opens the way to the experience of the "call of being," that is, of meaning as unconcealedness.

From all this we draw the conclusion that thinking about be-ing and "no-thing" is for Heidegger the road to the phenomenological reduction, which makes man's thinking find again its "element." According to Heidegger, traditional metaphysics has always reflected upon be-ing as be-ing; it has always claimed to mirror the "in itself." Thus the road to an authentic understanding of being, of meaning as unconcealedness, was blocked. The "brute" reality of the "in itself," however, is "nothing." The recognition of its "no-thingness" opens the road to the experience of the "truth of being."[47]

---

[44] Joseph Möller, *Existenzialphilosophie und katholische Theologie,* Baden-Baden, 1952, p. 139.

[45] Heidegger, *Was ist Metaphysik ?*, pp. 45-46.

[46] "Das Denken, dessen Gedanken nicht nur nicht rechnen, sondern überhaupt aus dem Anderen des Seienden bestimmt sind, heisse das wesentliche Denken. Statt mit dem Seienden auf das Seiende zu rechnen, verschwendet es sich im Sein für die Wahrheit des Seins." Heidegger, *ibid.,* p. 49.

[47] "Das Nichts ist das Nichts des Seienden und so das vom Seienden her erfahrene Sein. Die ontologische Differenz ist das Nichts zwischen Seiendem und Sein." Heidegger, *Vom Wesen des Grundes,* Frankfurt a.M., 3rd. ed., 1955, Vorwort zur dritten Auflage, p. 5.

The Meaning of the Greek "Physis"

At the first beginning of Western thought among the old Greek philosophers of "nature," Heidegger says, meaning was called "physis."[48] This Greek term received its Latin translation as "natura," and in the process lost its original meaning. The original inspiration of Greek philosophy perished at the same time.[49]

What, we may ask, was the original sense of "physis"? It expresses that which manifests itself in its unfolding,[50] the emergent. As such it can be observed, for example, in the rising of the sun, the rolling of the sea, the growth of plants, the coming forth of man and animal from the womb. By calling all this "physis," the Greeks did not want to say that these events were phenomena of "nature" in the sense which we now attach to this term. "Physis is being itself,"[51] that is, the coming out of concealedness, the being-unconcealed, the being-meaning of meaning. The Greeks did not learn through phenomena of "nature" what "physis" is, but, on the contrary, their fundamental feeling for what they called "physis" made them pay attention to phenomena of "nature" in the more restricted sense.[52] According to Heidegger, then, "physis" means to emerge, to come forth from concealment, to reveal itself, to endure as "revealed" and to "domin-

---

[48] Heidegger, *Einführung in die Metaphysik,* p. 10.

[49] "Der Vorgang dieser Uebersetzung des Griechischen ins Römische ist nichts Beliebiges und Harmloses, sondern der erste Abschnitt des Verlaufs der Abriegelung und Entfremdung des ursprünglichen Wesens der Griechischen Philosophie." Heidegger, *ibid.,* pp. 10-11.

[50] Heidegger, *ibid.,* p. 11.

[51] Heidegger, p. 11.

[52] "Erst auf Grund dieser Erschliessung konnten sie dann einen Blick haben für die Natur im engeren Sinne." Heidegger, *ibid.,* p. 11.

ate."[53] This "power of emerging and enduring" (*das aufgehende Walten*)[54] is being itself.

This original Greek inspiration was lost when "physis" was translated as "natura." For us, living in the technological age, that original meaning is completely forgotten. When we hear the term "nature," we think at once of nature as the physicist regards it, as motions of material things, as atoms and electrons. From the standpoint of our knowledge of physics, the Greeks appear to have been extremely primitive philosophers of "nature," at least if we understand their "physis" as "nature for the physicist."[55]

As a matter of fact, however, Heidegger continues, the Greeks' thinking was not primitive at all. The view that it was primitive forgets that what the Greeks wanted was philosophy, which is one of man's few great accomplishments. But what is great can only begin great and perish great. With Aristotle Greek thinking perished in greatness after its great beginning in the old Greek philosophers of "nature."[56] That beginning was not primitive, for the Greek philosophers of "nature" did not speak of "nature for the physicist" but of being as meaning.

We do not need to ask here whether Heidegger's interpretation of the Greek "physis" as being itself, conceived as the "power of emerging and enduring," is correct. For we are interested in what Heidegger himself means with being and with the "forgetfulness of being" of which he accuses traditional metaphysics. His interpretation of the

---

53 "*Phusis* ist das *Ent-stehen*, aus dem Verborgenen sich heraus- und dieses so erst in den Stand bringen." Heidegger, *ibid.*, p. 12.

54 Heidegger, *ibid.*, pp. 11-12.

55 "Die Griechen werden so im Grundsatz zu einer besseren Art von Hottentotten, denen gegenüber die neuzeitliche Wissenschaft unendlich weit fortgeschritten ist." Heidegger, *ibid.*, p. 12.

56 Heidegger, *ibid.*, pp. 12-13.

Greek "physis" is very illuminating in this matter. "Forgetfulness of being," the disregard of being, implies for Heidegger that traditional metaphysics neglected to pay attention to the fact that meaning is meaning. It simply took meaning as unconcealedness for granted and failed to realize that the emergence of appearing being is really the wonder of all wonders. It did not reflect upon meaning in its relationship to man, for whom and through whom alone meaning can appear, but "represented" meaning as being what it "is," as "brute" reality, as an "in itself." At the inception of Greek thought, Heidegger says, this was not yet the case. Only later did man "forget" meaning as unconcealedness. For this reason metaphysics must take a "step back."

The Interpretation of Being and Be-ing

We interrupt our argument here briefly to say a few words about the interpretation of Heidegger's being and be-ing. The claim that Heidegger's distinction between be-ing and being refers to the difference between the "brute" reality of the natural attitude and the meaning disclosed by the phenomenological reduction should not be interpreted as if nothing else remains to be said about his idea of being. Undoubtedly, it is true that Heidegger's train of thought from be-ing to being opened up for him the approach to the "in itself for us" of phenomenology. It was his way of overcoming the natural attitude. Albert Dondeyne also interprets Heidegger's "ontological difference" in this fashion.[57] He, too, remains silent about the further content of Heidegger's theory of being, although his silence is not at all meant to suggest that nothing else remains to be said. Alphonse de Waelhens makes use of this additional content in his own philoso-

---

[57] A. Dondeyne, "La différence ontologique chez M. Heidegger," *Revue philosophique de Louvain*, vol. LVI (1958), pp. 35-62, 251-293.

phy, but adds that he abstracts from the question whether his way of doing it is in harmony with Heidegger's intentions.[58]

It cannot be denied that Heidegger's theory of being contains more than we have indicated above. For, even after making the phenomenological reduction, Heidegger continues to distinguish between be-ing and being, but no longer in the sense of the difference between meaning and "brute" reality. After the phenomenological reduction has been made, he calls meaning again "be-ing" and says again that being is not be-ing.[59] Being and be-ing belong together, for being is never without be-ing, just as be-ing is not without being.[60] Nevertheless, being and be-ing are not entirely identical: appearance is not that which appears,[61] presence is not that which is present.[62] If, in the spirit of Heidegger's thinking, one wants to call the appearing of the thing its "thinging,"[63] and the appearing of the world the "worlding" of the world,[64] this "thinging" and this "worlding" cannot be identified with, respectively, the thing and the world. In the same line of thought, the being of be-ing cannot be identified

---

[58] A. De Waelhens, *La philosophie et les expériences naturelles,* p. 198, note.

[59] "Ob (das Seiende) und wie (das Seiende) erscheint . . . entscheidet nicht der Mensch. Die Ankunft des Seienden beruht im Geschick des Seins." Heidegger, *Ueber den Humanismus,* p. 19.

[60] ". . . dass das Sein nie west ohne das Seiende, dass niemals ein Seiendes ist ohne das Sein." Heidegger, *Was ist Metaphysik ?,* p. 46.

[61] "Indem nach dem Erscheinen als solchem gefragt wird, wird über die Sphäre der Erscheinung hinausgegangen. Die Phänomenalität der Phänomene ist kein phänomenales Problem." E. Fink, *Sein, Wahrheit, Welt,* p. 51.

[62] "Mais ce qui est présent ne peut être confondu avec la présence." De Waelhens, *op. cit.,* p. 198.

[63] Heidegger, *Vorträge und Aufsätze,* p. 172.

[64] Heidegger, *Holzwege,* Frankfurt a.M., 2nd ed., 1950, p. 33.

with be-ing, even though being and be-ing belong together.[65]

The objection could be raised that Heidegger explicitly states: "Being *is* be-ing." However, this expression does not permit us to identify being and be-ing in Heidegger, for he uses the term "is" here in a "transitive sense," to express that being "gathers" be-ing together insofar as it is be-ing.[66]

Accordingly, the "ontological difference" has more than a single sense in Heidegger. One of these senses is the distinction between the "brute" reality of the natural attitude and meaning in the phenomenological sense. This sense has been greatly emphasized in the preceding pages, while a second sense has merely been mentioned. It would be wrong to regard this procedure as a sign that from the standpoint of metaphysics we attach no importance to Heidegger's distinction between being and be-ing as he handles it after making the phenomenological reduction. However, we want to abstain from examining that importance here because it would lead us too far afield from our primary purpose, which is the consideration of the realism of phenomenology versus the realism of traditional metaphysics.

---

[65] "Sogar schon die Beziehung zwischen Anwesen und Anwesendem bleibt ungedacht. Von früh an scheint es, als sei das Anwesen und das Anwesende je etwas für sich. Unversehens wird das Anwesen selbst zu einem Anwesenden. Vom Anwesenden her vorgestellt, wird es zu dem über alles Anwesende her und so zum höchsten Anwesenden. Wenn das Anwesen genannt wird, ist schon Anwesendes vorgestellt. Im Grunde wird das Anwesen als ein solches gegen das Anwesende nicht unterschieden." Heidegger, *ibid,* pp. 335-336.

[66] "Das Sein ist das Seiende. Hierbei spricht 'ist' transitiv und besagt soviel wie 'versammelt'. Das Sein versammelt das Seiende darin, dass es Seiendes ist." Heidegger, *Was ist das - die Philosophie ?,* p. 22.

Nihilism and "Forgetfulness of Being"

We must now draw attention to the fact that Heidegger speaks about nihilism and forgetfulness of being both in connection with the neglect of the distinction between be-ing and be-ing in metaphysics[67] and in reference to the dictatorship of the sciences.[68] To overcome this nihilism and forgetfulness, Heidegger demands that thinking take a "step back." Man's thinking must return from metaphysics to the essence, the origin of metaphysics,[69] and from the technocratic mentality to the essence, the origin of technology. This twofold demand gives rise to the impression that the dictatorship of technology and the neglect of the distinction between be-ing and being are identified by him. Another factor serves to strengthen that impression: Heidegger calls the "step back from metaphysics" also the "step back toward the essence of technology."[70] Accordingly, he understands the be-ing traditionally considered by metaphysics as the "in itself," the "brute" reality of the natural attitude, which, in his view, metaphysics also has conceived in the way it is represented in the pursuit of the technical sciences. For, metaphysics wanted to be a science.[71]

Thus we see that Heidegger's thinking wants to protest against two fundamental theses of the natural attitude:

---

[67] "Die Seinsvergessenheit ist die Vergessenheit des Unterschieds des Seins zum Seienden." Heidegger, *Holzwege*, p. 336.

[68] Heidegger, *Zur Seinsfrage, passim.*

[69] "Der Schritt zurück bewegt sich daher aus der Metaphysik in das Wesen der Metaphysik." Heidegger, *Identität und Differenz*, p. 47.

[70] "Der Schritt zurük aus der Metaphysik in das Wesen der Metaphysik ist . . . der Schritt aus der Technologie und technologischen Beschreibung und Deutung des Zeitalters in das erst zu denkende *Wesen* der modernen Technik." Heidegger, *ibid.*, p. 48.

[71] Heidegger, *Ueber den Humanismus*, p. 6.

1. knowledge is a mirroring of "brute" reality; and 2. *the* system of objective mirrorings is the system of the sciences. The transcendence of metaphysics is brought about by substituting "existential" thinking for "representative" thinking, and this substitution leads us "back to the things themselves."

The "Step Back"

The "step back," the return from technology to the essence of technology as well as from metaphysics to the essence of metaphysics, is brought about, according to Heidegger, by replacing "representative" thinking by "thoughtful, 'existential' thinking." Existential thinking, as we have seen, is not a mirroring of be-ing as "brute" reality, but a dwelling with the truth of being as unconcealedness. It means paying attention to that which "is" (*west*), which is present (*an-west*), which unveils and manifests itself.[72] It is "dwelling" in, being present to, familiar with being, as that which concerns man.[73] The "step back" is a return to "existential" thinking as the genuine essence of man,[74] to *Dasein* which, as standing in the truth of being, lets being speak to itself.[75]

Heidegger calls "existential" thinking "an occurrence of being,"[76] and *Dasein* the "place" where being "occurs," or rather, where the "occurrence" of the truth of

---

[72] Heidegger, *Vorträge und Aufsätze,* p. 142.

[73] Heidegger, *Identität und Differenz,* p. 23.

[74] "Das ekstatische Innestehen im Offenen der Ortschaft des Seins ist als Verhältnis zum Sein . . . das Wesen des Denkens." Heidegger, *Nietzsche,* vol. II, p. 358.

[75] "Das Denken . . . lässt sich vom Sein in den Anspruch nehmen, um die Wahrheit des Seins zu sagen." Heidegger, *Ueber den Humanismus,* p. 5.

[76] "Wohl dagegen ist das wesentliche Denken ein Ereignis des Seins." Heidegger, *Was ist Metaphysik ?,* p. 47.

being is brought about by man's thinking. To make the truth of being "occur" is equiprimordially the self-unfolding, the self-development, the self-perfection of man's essence.[77] The fact that the truth of being "says" something to man, interests him and gives him "something to think" means that man is authentically man.[78]

To understand these Heideggerian statements one must keep in mind that the truth to which he refers here should not be conceived as the truth of propositions or judgments.[79] The truth of a judgment is based upon truth in a more primordial sense, viz., truth as the unconcealedness of that to which the proposition refers.[80] If we ask what makes that which is unconcealed unconcealed, the reply is that unconcealedness is brought about by the "dis-closure" of *Dasein*. This dis-closure consists in *Dasein's* letting being be what it is.[81] This "letting be" is *Dasein* itself, as "dis-closure," as the "unconcealing" of being. Dis-closing something, however, is an "event," and for this reason Heidegger says that truth "occurs" as the unconcealedness of being. The "occurring" and "being brought about" of the truth of being is the self-unfolding and self-development of *Dasein* as "thoughtful" thinking, as the "existential" thinking, through which be-

---

77 "Der Anspruch des Seins räumt den Menschen erst in sein Wesen ein." Heidegger, *Der Satz vom Grund,* p. 119; Heidegger, *Ueber den Humanismus,* pp. 5-6.

78 "Die Metaphysik verschliesst sich dem einfachen Wesensbestand, dass der Mensch nur in seinem Wesen west, in dem er vom Sein angesprochen wird." Heidegger, *Ueber den Humanismus,* p. 13.

79 Heidegger, *Vom Wesen der Wahrheit,* Frankfurt a.M., 1954, p. 7.

80 Heidegger, *ibid.,* pp. 14-15.

81 "Die Freiheit zum Offenbaren eines Offenen lässt das jeweilige Seiende das Seiende sein, das es ist. Freiheit enthüllt sich jetzt als das Seinlassen von Seiendem." Heidegger, *ibid.,* p. 14.

ing is "the affair of thinking."[82]

To overcome the "forgetfulness of being" which characterizes traditional metaphysics, man must return, says Heidegger, to the essence, the origin of metaphysics. This return consists in a revaluation of "existential" thinking, which points to *Dasein* as "standing in the light of being." Being enlightens, is unconcealed by the "letting be" of *Dasein*. Being is that which as present (*Anwesen*),[83] as appearing (*Erscheinen*),[84] concerns man.

Traditional metaphysics, says Heidegger, has always neglected to pay attention to this point. It has always taken be-ing as be-ing for granted and acted as if the appearing of be-ing did not raise any problems. It assumed the "natural attitude."[85] The be-ing spoken of by traditional metaphysics evidently is the be-ing that has already appeared.[86] But this metaphysics forgets that the be-ing of which it speaks is the be-ing that has already appeared. Hence it suffers from "forgetfulness of being." Its forgetfulness became forgetfulness of being precisely because it "forgot" that it "had forgotten."[87]

Metaphysics did not reflect upon be-ing in its appearing, in relation to *Dasein*, but represented be-ing as an "in itself."[88] Metaphysics is without ground because it

---

[82] Heidegger, *Identität und Differenz,* p. 37.

[83] Heidegger, *Zur Seinsfrage,* p. 28.

[84] Heidegger, *Vorträge und Aufsätz,* p. 142.

[85] Dondeyne, "La différence ontologique chez M. Heidegger," *loc. cit.* (footnote 57), p. 44.

[86] Dondeyne, *ibid.,* p. 61.

[87] Heidegger, *Nietzsche,* vol. II, p. 360.

[88] "Die Metaphysik fragt nicht nach der Wahrheit des Seins selbst. Sie fragt daher auch nie, in welcher Weise das Wesen des Menschen zur Wahrheit des Seins gehört. Diese Frage hat die Metaphysik nicht nur bisher nicht gestellt. Diese Frage ist der Metaphysik als Metaphysik unzugänglich." Heidegger, *Vom Wesen der Wahrheit,* pp. 12-13.

neglected the origin of metaphysics in *Dasein*. The question about being is for Heidegger the question about the origin of the truth of being as unconcealedness and therefore the question about the ground of metaphysics. To transcend metaphysics by the "step back" toward its essence is to transcend the natural attitude and to perform the phenomenological reduction. The be-ing considered by metaphysics was conceived as "brute" reality, as an "in itself."[89] The being which comes to light by transcending metaphysics is meaning in the phenomenological sense of the "in itself for us."

Heidegger adds explicitly that being is not God and not the cause of the world.[90] Within the context of his terminology it could not be otherwise. Being is for him the correlate of "existential" thinking conceived as "encounter." Being is that which man's thinking "hears" after making the phenomenological reduction.[91] It is that which is present, that which comes immediately to light for *Dasein*, that which imposes itself as "present reality" to the existent subject-as-*Cogito*. But God is not present in that way, and for this reason Heidegger correctly emphasizes that what he calls being is not God. His denial, however, does not mean that Heidegger denies God.

---

[89] "Assurément, 'être' a toujours pour l'homme un sens humain, seulement nous sommes facilement enclins à penser qu'un discours *vrai* est celui qui parle des étants tels qu'ils sont 'en soi', indépendamment de toute référence au mode d'existence qui est nôtre." Dondeyne, *loc. cit.* (footnote 57), p. 57.

[90] "Das 'Sein' - das ist nicht Gott und nicht ein Weltgrund." Heidegger, *Ueber den Humanismus*, p. 19.

[91] "Was das Denken als Vernehmen vernimmt, ist das Präsente in seiner Präsenz. An ihr nimmt das Denken das Mass für sein Wesen als Vernehmen. Demgemäss ist das Denken jene Präsentation des Präsenten, die uns das Anwesende in seiner Anwesenheit zu-stellt und es damit vor uns stellt, damit wir vor dem Anwesenden stehen und innerhalb seiner dieses Stehen ausstehen können." Heidegger, *Vorträge und Aufsätze*, p. 141.

It merely expresses the conviction that God cannot be encountered by "existential" thinking as an immediately present reality.[92] In other words, it decides nothing whatsoever either positively or negatively with respect to God. Nevertheless, the substitution of authentic thinking for "representative" thinking places man on a standpoint from which the question about God can be raised in a meaningful way.[93]

According to Heidegger, being is "closer to man than is any be-ing, regardless of whether the latter is a rock, an animal, a work of art, a machine, an angel or God."[94] Some Thomists object to the inclusion of God in this list of examples because it puts God on the same line as other be-ings. God, they say, is not a be-ing (*ens*) but Being itself (*ipsum esse*), Subsistent Being. Thomism at least, they add, does not represent God as a be-ing.[95] This criticism would be to the point if Heidegger's terminology were the same as that of St. Thomas. But Heidegger's be-ing and being are not the be-ing (*ens*) and being (*esse*) of Aquinas. If, then, Heidegger enumerates God among his be-ings, he does not consider Him as one of the Thomistic be-ings (*entia*). For Heidegger, be-ing means "brute" reality. By placing God together with oth-

---

[92] M. Müller, *Existenzphilosophie im geistigen Leben der Gegenwart*, Heidelberg, 1949, pp. 73-74.

[93] Heidegger, *Vom Wesen des Grundes*, Frankfurt a.M., 4th ed., 1955, p. 39.

[94] "Das Sein ist . . . näher als jedes Seiende, sei dies ein Fels, ein Tier, ein Kunstwerk, ein Maschine, sei es ein Engel oder Gott. Das Sein ist das Nächste." Heidegger, *Ueber den Humanismus*, pp. 19-20.

[95] "Nach dem *Theismus* hingegen ist Gott nie dem Sein unter- und dem Seienden gleichgeordnet, kommt ihm das höchste und unvergleichlich eigentliche 'ist' zu, vereinigt er die ganze Fülle des Seins ursprünglich in sich und ist deshalb nicht ein Seiendes, sondern *Ipsum Esse*, das Sein *selbst* oder das *subsistierende Sein*." Lotz, "Heidegger und das Sein," *Universitas*, vol. VI (1951), p. 840.

er examples of be-ings, Heidegger does not lower Him to a be-ing in the Thomistic sense, an *ens*, but simply expresses that traditional metaphysics has also represented the Subsistent Being as "brute" reality, as an "in itself." In other words, traditional thinking about God has been unable to overcome the natural attitude. Who would dare to claim that Heidegger's complaint in this matter is false?

"No" Metaphysics?

Heidegger himself has explicitly stated that man's thinking which tries to penetrate into the ground of metaphysics is not itself a form of metaphysics.[96] "Metaphysics as such is nihilism in the proper sense."[97] Within the context of Heidegger's ideas this statement makes sense. For, if metaphysics is characterized by thinking in the natural attitude, any form of thinking which transcends the natural attitude through the phenomenological reduction cannot be called "metaphysics" in the same sense as thinking in the natural attitude.

Although Heidegger's intention in using this terminology is sufficiently clear, his words can easily be misunderstood. The same must be said of the way in which many phenomenologists speak when they object to certain views concerning "scientific," "rational" or "objective" thinking. They take exception to scientistic, rationalistic and objectivistic excesses and, on the basis of their legitimate objections, say that phenomenological thinking is not scientific, not rational, not objective. But they object also when others, as could be expected, conclude that phenomenological thinking is unscientific, irrational and subjectivistic.

---

96 Heidegger, *Was ist Metaphysik ?*, p. 21.

97 Heidegger, *Nietzsche*, vol. II, p. 350.

Such difficulties can easily be avoided. Heidegger's thinking, as a return to the ground of metaphysics, may certainly be called metaphysical, be it not a metaphysical thinking in the natural attitude.[98] *De facto* Heidegger made the "step back" from metaphysics to the ground of metaphysics as early as his *Being and Time*. Yet in this book he called his thinking still metaphysics, and correctly so. Later he introduced a different terminology, but this new way of referring to his thinking does not change its character.[99]

As should be evident from the preceding considerations, Heidegger is concerned with the question about the realism of traditional metaphysics. Realism, or rather, the absence of an authentic realism in phenomenology, is the stumbling block of many metaphysicians. In the following section we must now consider this question explicitly.

2. *Traditional Metaphysics and Realism*

The Traditional Formulation of the Metaphysical Question and Phenomenology

"Why is there something rather than nothing?" This formulation of the metaphysical question comes from Leibnitz. It expresses in a very precise fashion in what exactly the metaphysical question in the strict sense is interested. The question is concerned with the meaning of something as something, as not-nothing; it is interested in be-ing as be-ing, as not nonbe-ing. The question aims at the totality, the universality of be-ing as be-ing.

This question, obviously, cannot be regarded as a specific question arising from a particular attitude of the existent subject-as-*Cogito just as* other questions are specific questions and other attitudes are particular attitudes.

---

98 Heidegger, *ibid.,* vol. II, p. 350.

99 Müller, *op. cit.,* pp. 56-57.

On the contrary, in the metaphysical question we have to do with an all-encompassing attitude of questioning and with the all-encompassing character of meaning as meaning. The metaphysical question does not put a specific region of being, as distinct from other regions, on the foreground of the field of presence considered by the existent subject-as-*Cogito*. The reason is that it does not ask about a particular specific meaning but about meaning as meaning. Only nothing is distinct from meaning as meaning, and therefore only nothing limits the field of presence considered by the subject who raises the metaphysical question.

The questions which metaphysics as a science raises explicitly take up and develop the metaphysical "awareness," the metaphysical "experience" which the subject-as-*Cogito* himself is. Thanks to the subject's emergence from the endless evolution of the cosmos, there is meaning for man because the subject is the "natural light" that is presupposed by all meaning.[100] The occurrence of the subject's emergence is at the same time the "occurrence," the emergence of human truth as unconcealedness.[101] The truth of meaning presupposes the constituting activity of the subject as "natural light." (Since we are speaking here of the subject-as-*Cogito*, we could say the "unveiling activity" instead of the "constituting activity.") The subject, however, is an intentional, an existent subject; the subject is not separated from the meaning but immediately present to it. As intentionality, as "existence," the subject is a kind of "being in," "being familiar with," "inhabiting," "being present to" meaning as that which is un-

---

[100] Heidegger, *Sein und Zeit,* p. 133.

[101] "Il y a métaphysique à partir du moment où, cessant de vivre dans l'évidence de l'objet - qu'il s'agisse de l'objet sensoriel ou de l'objet de la science - nous apercevons indissolublement la subjectivé radicale de toute notre expérience et sa valeur de vérité." Merleau-Ponty, *Sens et Non-sens,* pp. 186-187.

mistakably present[102] and of which must be said: "It *is*." This "saying" is the subject himself.

It stands to reason that this "saying" should not be conceived as an explicit act of judgment. The judgment is an intentional act which presupposes the "functioning intentionality" which the subject-as-*Cogito* himself is. This "functioning intentionality" constantly "says": "It is." If this most primordial and implicit "saying" of being is thought away, every judgment loses its meaning. For, every judgment expresses that this or that *is* this way or that way, and, by removing the most primordial "saying" of being, one removes also the source of the explicit affirmation of what is. It remains possible, of course, to state in a *purely verbal* fashion that things "are" even without the subject. However, such a statement acquires an intelligible meaning and thereby becomes a genuine statement only if the supposition that there is no subject is *not really* made.

Accordingly, Husserl's demand that philosophy go "back to the things themselves" implies not only a return to the world in which man lives as the most primordial ground of all objectivity; it implies not only a recognition of intentionality as man's access to objectivity; but it contains also a vision of the intentional subject as the most primordial "saying" of being, with respect to which all judgments are explicitations.

The metaphysical affirmation is contained as a specific moment in this most primordial "saying" of being. It is an aspect of being-man and therefore any metaphysics presupposes a philosophical anthropology and epistemology.

---

[102] "La présence et ce qui est présent ne sont pas *seulement* opposés; une corrélation non moins radicale que leur opposition les rend, tout autant qu'opposés, inséparables. En soi, si l'on ose ainsi s'exprimer, l'étant n'a aucune référence au sens ou à la présence." De Waelhens, *La philosophie et les expériences naturelles*, p. 199.

These two impress their mark upon metaphysics, and for this reason it is possible that one metaphysician will reproach the other as not being authentically metaphysical.

In the preceding paragraphs we have emphasized that the traditional question about the meaning of be-ing as be-ing easily fits into a phenomenological anthropology and epistemology. To recognize that this question is legitimate does not require the denial of intentionality, for the question itself must be conceived as an aspect of that intentionality, namely, as man's "dwelling" in the universality of being. To recognize the legitimate character of the traditional metaphysical question likewise does not demand that one deny the phenomenological reduction, for be-ing and the universe are not conceived as "in themselves" but as clinging to the subject as finding and placing himself in a "special" attitude. Finally, the traditional questions of metaphysics do not imply the denial of the primordial "saying" of being which the existent subject-as-*Cogito* is. For, obviously, even if one claims that there is a universe without the subject, that very claim can be *really* made only because one does *not really* make the supposition that there is no subject.

There are phenomenologists who think that a phenomenological inspiration of thinking makes it impossible to ask about be-ing as be-ing. They believe that this question demands the denial of intentionality and disregarding of the phenomenological reduction. As is evident from the preceding pages, we do not agree with them. Yet it is easy to see why these phenomenologists hold that view. For within traditional metaphysics intentionality and the phenomenological reduction are not considered. The questions of traditional metaphysics are raised from the standpoint of the natural attitude. Hence it stands to reason that one who takes up the questions of traditional metaphysics assumes the natural attitude and thereby denies intentionality and the phenomenological reduction.

We have explicitly tried to make room for the questions of traditional metaphysics within the theory of intentionality and the phenomenological reduction. This, however, is also the reason why some metaphysicians accuse phenomenology of not being, and being unable to be, metaphysics, for in their view intentionality and the phenomenological reduction make realism impossible. The presence or absence of realism, they claim, decides whether a particular form of metaphysical thinking is authentic, is what it ought to be. Realism, they maintain, is absent from phenomenology. In this sense they accuse phenomenology of being unable to inquire into be-ing as be-ing. Phenomenology, they allege, cannot ask the metaphysical question in the realistic sense, in the only sense in which the question ought to be asked to be *really* a question.

Obviously, everything depends here on the sense given to the term "realism." Heidegger's ideas about metaphysics and his objections against it again can serve to throw light upon this question.

The Accepted Sense of Realism

The accepted sense of realism is the realism of the natural attitude. It is not possible to describe this realism without lapsing into the contradictions inherent in it. They have to be accepted in the description, in the hope that the nonsensical character of this realism becomes unambiguously clear.

In the natural attitude knowledge is not conceived as the immediate presence of a human subject to a present reality, but as the mirroring, in a worldless subject, of things that are separate from the subject. In the natural attitude the "encounter," the unity of reciprocal implication of subject and object, is broken. The object, which with all its meanings is and remains nonetheless object-for-a-subject, is "realized,"[103] that is, it is represented as "real," as being separate from the subject-as-*Cogito*, and as being "in itself" that which it is in true knowledge for the subject.

Within knowledge conceived as "encounter" grass reveals itself as green, ice as cold, a fish as slippery, a knife as sharp, a wall as solid, a mountain chain as inaccessible, Mt. McKinley as high, Sirius as distant, water as thirst-quenching, as salty, as H_2O or as extinguishing fire. Within knowledge as "encounter" a chair reveals itself as a piece of furniture to sit on, a hammer as an instrument for carpentry, a soccer club as a milieu for recreation, a state as an economic, social and political society, loyalty as ethically good, hatred and murder as ethically evil.

These meanings, we have said, reveal themselves within the "encounter" which knowledge is. As such, they are the result of a long, personal and collective, intentional history of the subject-as-*Cogito*. This subject, to speak with Heidegger, as "dis-closure" (*Entbergung*) lets meaning be what it is, shows himself sensitive to meaning, lets meaning speak to him and be his norm. In the natural attitude, however, the meaning is cut loose from the encounter and "posited," "represented" and "affirmed" as "in itself," that is, as something that is, separately from the intentional subject, eternal and immutable. In other words, the fact that meaning is a "result" is forgotten. One places oneself on a standpoint prior to the beginning of the personal and collective history of dis-closure and nevertheless "affirms" that the "mean-

---

103 "Pour la première fois, la méditation du philosophe est assez consciente pour ne pas réaliser dans le monde et avant elle ses propres résultats." Merleau-Ponty, *Phénoménologie de la perception,* p. XV.

ing" as an "in itself" is eternally and immutably that which it reveals itself to be in true knowledge.

The contradictions necessary to describe this form of realism are evident. Meaning has to be presented as an "in itself," as separate from the subject-as-*Cogito*. Divorced from the subject, however, who is the "natural light," meaning is pure concealedness, unspeakable chaos, impenetrable darkness.[104] Even these descriptive terms are contradictions, for they also presuppose the subject and do not describe an "in itself." Meaning cannot be really "represented," "posited" and "affirmed" unless there is a subject who represents, posits and affirms. One can claim that in realism the world is "represented" as a world exhibition or as a spectacle, but all such expressions are bereft of sense without the spectator. Yet this spectator is precisely what has to be removed to emphasize what the "in itself" is. Without getting involved in contradiction, the form of realism to which we are referring here and which is the accepted form cannot be described. For the "in itself" is the not-known, the non-affirmed, the not-represented be-ing. How could anyone know, affirm or represent such a be-ing?[105] Any representation of the "in itself" is "hypocritical" and naive for, without mentioning it, it presupposes the subject-as-*Cogito* through whom a world arranges itself around the

---

104 "Sans le 'réel', il n'y aurait rien; sans le sujet ou la transcendancee, il n'y aurait que le plein d'un indicible chaos, le nonsens absolu, c'est-à-dire encore rien." De Waelhens, *La philosophie et les expériences naturelles,* (La Haye, 1961) p. 186.

105 "Il va de soi que ce langage ne peut être pris à la lettre. En rigueur de termes, rien ne peut être 'dit' de l'étant que le surgissement de l'homme n'aurait pas encore élevé à la présence, puisque tout parole relève de la présence. Le qualifier d' 'étant,' d' 'en-soi', etc . . ., c'est déjà l' 'illuminer'." De Waelhens, *ibid.,* p. 199, note.

subject and begins to be for the subject.[106]

Sometimes this form of realism is also called "objectivism"[107] or "essentialism." The most widely used term, however, is "representative realism." We must now see why it is called by this name.

Knowledge as Mirroring

One who does not conceive knowledge as the immediate presence of the subject-as-*Cogito* to a present reality can hardly escape defining it as mirroring. He has broken contact with meaning and "forgotten" that meaning is the result of a long intentional history, a long history of dis-closing contact. Yet when he wants to speak about knowledge, he can not escape speaking about a kind of "contact." Since a direct and real contact by means of immediate presence is excluded, it is replaced by contact through mirror images, "depicting ideas" (Descartes), "impressions" (Locke), or "impressed species" (Scholastics) which are supposed to represent the "in itself."[108] Through its mirror images the "in itself" acquires being for the subject-as-*Cogito*, but this being is not the meaning itself, distinct from the subject, but the appearance of the "in itself" in the "internal world" of the sub-

---

[106] *Phénoménologie de la perception*, p. III; De Waelhens, *ibid.*, pp. 190-191.

[107] De Waelhens, *ibid.*, p. 190.

[108] "Puisqu'un tableau nous fait penser à ce qu'il représente, on supposera, en se fondant sur le cas privilégié des appareils visuels, que les sens reçoivent des choses réelles de 'petits tableaux' qui excitent l'ame à les percevoir. Les 'simulacres' épicuriens ou les 'espèces intentionnelles,' 'toutes ces petites images voltigeantes par l'air' qui apportent dans le corps l'aspect sensible des choses, ne font que transporter en termes d'explication causale et d'opérations réelles la présence idéale de la chose au sujet percevant qui, nous l'avons vu, est une évidence pour la conscience naive." Merleau-Ponty, *La structure du comportement*, Paris, 3rd ed., 1953, p. 205.

ject-as-*Cogito*. A kind of duplication of the "in itself" takes place, and through it the subject has a guarantee of being in "contact" with the object of knowledge. This contact, then, is a mirroring.

The difficulties of realism become even greater through this theory of knowledge. For the very possibility to speak of true knowledge is now absolutely and definitively eliminated. In the perspective of representative realism the statement that knowledge is true knowledge means that the subject "really" mirrors the "in itself." Differently expressed, it means that being for the subject is in agreement with "being in itself," that is, with not being for the subject. But who would be able to affirm that agreement? To affirm it, one would have to make a comparison between, on the one hand, something that is for the subject, and on the other, something that "is," i.e., is not for the subject.

Heidegger's reproach to Western thought applies to this kind of realism. It lives in "forgetfulness of being," for it has neglected to reflect upon meaning as unconcealedness and upon the subject as "letting be" and as "speech." This forgetfulness is without remedy as long as man's thinking remains within the natural attitude. The subject of knowledge is said to "possess" his object; at the same time the "in itself" is conceived as separate from the subject; hence, it is no longer possible to call the "in itself" the object of knowledge, for precisely the "in itself" is not "possessed" by the subject. If knowledge is conceived as mirroring, the subject "possesses" only the images or impressions of the things, so that ultimately these images have to be called the object of knowledge. Thus the *Cogito* can no longer in any way be explicitated as consciousness of the things themselves,[109] but only as

---

[109] "Das Raumding, das wir sehen, ist bei all seiner Transzendenz Wahrgenommenes, in seiner Leibhaftigkeit bewusstseins-

consciousness of the images of things.

The "forgetfulness of being" is now beyond remedy. Man's thinking is locked up in reflections upon phenomena (*Erscheinungen*). It becomes useless to search for a possibility to affirm and to know the "thing in itself," as that which is hidden behind the phenomena. For the "thing in itself" has been "defined" in advance by the natural attitude as the not-affirmed and the not-known. This "forgetfulness of being" can be eliminated only by renouncing the natural attitude and making the phenomenological reduction. However, such a renunciation would mean the death of representative realism.

Let us add that we have no objection against calling realism essential for an authentic metaphysics. This realism, however, cannot be the representative kind. One who considers representative realism essential for metaphysics should not address phenomenology with the reproach that it rejects metaphysics. For in that case it does not reject metaphysics but only a contradiction.

The Essentialism of Scholastic Metaphysics

Those who claim that the implications of the phenomenological reduction make realism impossible emphasize the necessity of stripping traditional realism of its passivism and of its representative interpretation.[110] They admit that traditional metaphysics is "too realistic and too objectivistic," and that this defect has been exposed by phenomenology. They demand that metaphysics be

---

mässig Gegebenes. Es ist nicht statt seiner ein Bild oder ein Zeichen gegeben. Man unterschiebe nicht dem Wahrnehmen ein Zeichen- oder Bildbewusstsein." Husserl, *Ideen*, vol. I, pp. 98-99.

[110] "At any rate, traditional realism must rid itself of its passivism and also of every representative interpretation." De Petter, *Metaphysiek en phaenomenologie*, p. 6.

radically purged of this defect,[111] and that it overcome the essentialism in which it has become entangled in its long history.[112]

Accordingly, scholastic philosophers themselves accuse metaphysics of what Heidegger calls "forgetfulness of be-ing." This accusation is not surprising. Reality is presented in scholasticism as a collection of essences assembled in a land whose discovery has never been reflected upon. The first preparation of that idea may be found in Plato. This Greek philosopher was struck by the aspect of necessity and universality in man's knowledge, but the heritage of Heraclitus made it impossible for him to find a foundation for that aspect in the world. He therefore conceived a separate world of necessary and universal ideas which, as pure essences, could be the prototypes of all worldly realities. This world of ideas was regarded as the universal and necessary norm by which all worldly realities, as shadows of ideas, could be measured and on the basis of which one could determine whether a given be-ing was a be-ing having this or that essence. The world of ideas contained, for example, the pure essence of the state, of the work of art, of man, of virtues, and of the horse. The ideas functioned as the measure of the "truth" of things. The concrete living human be-ing had nothing else to do than to realize his necessary, universal, immutable and eternal essence in changeable time.[113]

---

111 "The central ideas of phenomenology . . . have indeed revealed a serious defect in traditional metaphysics. The latter really did not pay sufficient attention to the central place occupied by man in the world; it was more interested in the theater in which the drama of human existence was played than in this drama itself. If traditional metaphysics wants to retain its appeal to modern man, it will have to rid itself radically of this defect." J. Plat, *Traditionele metafysiek en fenomenologie*, pp. 9-10.

112 De Petter, *op. cit.*, p. 9.

113 "So ist von vornherein festgelegt und erblickt, was der Mensch sein soll und sein muss. Ihm bleibt nichts anderes übrig,

Plato conceived the world of pure ideas as a world of pure "light." The pure idea is pure "light," in contrast to the meaning spoken of by phenomenology. Meaning is not pure "light" but a mixture of "light" and "darkness," of unconcealedness and concealment for the subject. The unconcealedness of meaning presupposes that the subject-as-*Cogito* lets the meaning be. The moment of the emergence of the subject-as-*Cogito* is the moment when truth as unconcealedness emerges. This moment is the beginning of a history of dis-closure which will never be finished. Meaning is never pure "light."

The fact that phenomenology conceives meaning as the chiaroscuro of unconcealedness and concealment makes it possible to call meaning the real term of encounter with respect to knowledge. Its *real* terms of encounter are a mixture of "light" and "darkness." When Plato conceived meaning as pure idea, as pure "light," he no longer conceived it as a real term of encounter. The Platonic idea, conceived as pure "light," must actually be regarded as the meaning whose moment of dis-closure is "forgotten" and whose history of dis-closure is considered finished. But for such a finished result there is no room within knowledge as real encounter, for in a real encounter with meaning the latter reveals itself as the chiaroscuro of unconcealedness and concealment, and consequently as a never-ending invitation to dis-closure by the subject-as-*Cogito*. Plato had to separate meaning from the encounter, to place it as an "in itself" of a purely ideal character in a world of pure essences.

In Aristotle's philosophy the essences were no longer conceived as existing in an ideal world but in the real world. He regarded the Platonic essence as an "in itself"

---

als Verwirklicher seines eigenen ewigen Wesens zu sein, seine unveränderliche, ihn ermöglichende innere Möglichkeit ins Dasein überzuführen." Müller, *op. cit.*, p. 17.

of an ideal nature but not as a term of encounter. Because Aristotle simply placed these essences in "reality," he implicitly conceived their "reality" also as an "in itself." In other words, he transferred the "in itself" from the ideal to the real world, but did not bring the essences back to their place within the encounter. Exactly like the Platonic essences, they were conceived as absolute "light," though not of an ideal but of a real character. Aristotle represented these essences as in themselves necessarily universally, immutably and eternally "true," for as absolute "light" they functioned as the norm of truth with respect to judgments. In this way reality was pictured as a collection of essences assembled in a land of absolute "light," but the history of the origin and growth of this light was never reflected upon.

The same view lies at the foundation of the hierarchic realism of the scholastics, which assigned to each essence its own place in "brute" reality. Man, with his own essence, was likewise assumed to have his place in that hierarchy,[114] a position below that of God but above animals, plants and things. The sacred had its place above the beautiful, the beautiful above the useful, the useful above the agreeable, the common above the individual, the soul above the body.[115] The essences of man's acts were likewise planted as rocks in the "totality of reality." They were assumed to be in their essences what they are: necessarily, universally, immutably and eternally "true"-in-themselves. The essence of the marriage act, for example, was conceived as in itself of necessity, universal-

---

[114] "L'objectivisme naturaliste . . . regarde . . . *l'omnitudo realitatis,* assigne à l'homme son rang . . . dans le spectacle qu'elle s'offre et néglige totalement de retenir que l'origine de cette hiérarchie réside dans l'activité législatrice du 'regard' de l'étant illuminateur du spectacle et qui le 'constitue' tel." De Waelhens, *op. cit.,* pp. 190-191.

[115] Müller, *op. cit.,* pp. 19-20.

ly, immutably and eternally orientated toward reproduction. This orientation was the "truth"-in-itself of the marriage act, the norm of every judgment concerning this act. Natural rights and natural obligations were planted as "hills and valleys" in the "totality of reality," as of necessity, universally, immutably and eternally "true"-in-themselves and therefore the norms of all judgments.

This view implied a special conception of man's ethical actions, which followed from the following three theses:

1. Immutable and eternal essences lie in ready-made assembly in the "totality of reality."

2. Immutable and eternal relationships constitute an immutable and eternal hierarchy of order among these essences.

3. Man and his actions have an immutable and eternal place in this whole of "truths"-in-themselves.

From these three theses it followed that the concrete man living in the concrete world ought to "read" the essences and their essential hierarchy and that his actions would be ethically good if they were in conformity with these essences and their hierarchy.[116]

By observing this conformity, man would accomplish the will of God. For, the scholastic philosophers did not merely transfer the Platonic ideas to the real world but also gave them, as exemplars of the real essences, a place in the intellect of God, who through a creative act of His will gave reality to these exemplars. "Truth"-in-themselves, therefore, was ascribed to these essences, and this

---

[116] "Für die Handlungen gibt es keine anderen Maxime als die: Beobachte den unveränderlichen *Ordo,* schütze ihn, wo er bedroht ist, stelle ihn her, wo er gestört ist, verwirkliche ihn dort, wo sein Gegenteil Wirklichkeit geworden und in die Möglichkeit zurückgesunken ist. Zu diesem *Ordo* gehört auch, dass du den Platz einnimmt, der dir auf Grund deines Wesens zukommt." Müller, *ibid.,* p. 20.

truth was measured and derived from their "truth" in the intellect of God: every be-ing is true.[117] To the extent that man's true knowledge mirrored the "truth"-in-itself of the essences, he possessed God's view of things.

In this way the essentialism, objectivism and realism of of scholastic philosophy reached its apex in the claim to speak about things in the name of God.[118] The difficulties become insurmountable, of course, as soon as one realizes that contradictions occur also among scholastic philosophers.

"Truth in Itself" and "Truth as a Human Possession"

Non-scholastic philosophers have presented the above-described portrait of scholastic thinking for the consideration of scholastic philosophers. The latter have recognized that the portrait is correct.[119] For this reason they now demand that scholastic realism strip itself of passivism and the representative interpretation of realism, because it is "too realistic and too objectivistic."[120]

It would be a mistake, however, to think that representative realism is ever "officially," explicitly or de-

---

117 L. Landgrebe, *Philosophie der Gegenwart,* Bonn, 1952, p. 157.

118 ". . . comme si la conscience humaine pouvait en quelque sorte se survoler elle-même et son monde, et contempler l'univers du point de vue de Dieu." Dondeyne, *loc. cit.* (footnote 57), p. 57.

119 "Such a way of representing matters impresses us today as evidently unreal." De Petter, *Metaphysiek en phaenomenologie,* p. 6.

120 "Traditional philosophy . . . has indeed usually represented matters as if man finds himself in a world of immutable essences and eternal truths, from which essences and truths he could 'read' the moral norms of his actions. It was man's task to decipher these essences, truths and norms by means of his intellect, to become familiar with them and to understand them to the best of his ability . . . He would then try to subject his will and his actions to these norms . . . That was what God had willed." De Petter, *ibid.,* p. 6.

liberately defended by scholastic thinkers. No one will ever deliberately pretend that he affirms, knows or speaks about non-affirmed, non-know or not-spoken-about reality. Representationism always remains a purely implicit conviction that is not acknowledged as a conviction. It lies implied in convictions which do not "officially" express representationism but nonetheless contain it of necessity. For this reason one should not be surprised to find it even among thinkers who explicitly reject the representative interpretation of realism. Anyone who realizes the contradictory character of representationism rejects it, of course, but this rejection does not necessarily mean that he does not continue to adhere to it implicitly.

Representationism remains implicitly present when someone makes a distinction between "truth in itself" and "truth as a human possession." The former, it is said, does not change, but the latter is subject to change. "Truth as a human possession" can change because man's grasp of truth is "perspectivistic," that is, it is a view of truth from a certain standpoint and therefore subject to growth and complementary additions. Man can never make definitive all-round statements. Only God from His absolute standpoint can do this. No one has a monopoly on truth. The fact, however, that man is aware of "perspectivism" shows that at the same time he transcends this perspectivism. By constantly varying his perspectives, he gradually comes closer to the one and absolute reality.

Phenomenology does not, of course, deny that perspectivism is overcome in the above-mentioned sense. However, if this undeniable transcendence is formulated in the distinction between "truth in itself" and "truth as a human possession," representative realism is surreptitiously re-introduced, in spite of its explicit rejection. For, what could be the meaning of the expression "truth in itself"? It obviously does not refer to the truth of the judgment since the latter is not primary but based on the unconcealedness of reality. If, however, "truth" has to be understood as unconcealedness, "truth in itself" would refer to "unconcealedness in itself." But what possible *real* content could be assigned to "unconcealedness in itself"? There is no room for it within knowledge conceived as encounter with meaning. This "unconcealedness in itself," moreover, is distinguished from "truth as a human possession," that is, from unconcealedness for man. Distinguishing these two means that one is said not to be the other. Hence "unconcealedness in itself" is not "unconcealedness for man." "Unconcealedness in itself" is, of course, not really encountered anywhere, for whatever is *really* encountered is encountered as unconcealed for man.

Accordingly, by speaking of "unconcealedness in itself," one places it outside the encounter which knowledge is. The historical moment of dis-closure, which makes all unconcealedness unconcealedness, is "forgotten." The "unconcealed in itself" is distinguished from the unconcealed that comes into man's possession by means of man's never finished, historical, perspectivistic grasping of reality. By positing "unconcealedness in itself," one claims that the history of dis-closure has reached its end and presents truth in itself as an absolute "light" . . . for no one.[121] Such a way of presenting matters is judged by scholastic philosophers themselves as "evidently unreal."

The perspectivism of human knowledge and man's awareness of it permit us, of course, to distinguish levels

---

[121] "Ce que nous refusons, parce que ce serait parler d'un sens avant le sens, c'est de partir, dans l'absolu, d'une vérité en soi et première de la chose ou des choses, c'est de croire que la naissance de l'humanité viendrait entériner ou modifier ou rendre caduque cette nature 'spectaculaire' de *l'omnitudo realitatis.*" De Waelhens, *op. cit.,* p. 98.

of knowledge. Such distinctions are made also by existential phenomenology.[122] However, these distinctions cannot be reduced to the opposition between immutable truth in itself and mutable truth as a human possession. Truth reveals itself as immutable inside man's grasp of it and not outside it. It reveals itself as immutable on many different levels.

Exactly the same difficulty, the inevitable lapse into representative realism, arises when the distinction between "truth in itself" and "truth as a human possession" is avoided and replaced by a distinction between "being itself" and "being for man." When this distinction is used, it may at first seem possible to forget that being is being-true. The seeming possibility to forget this point is important since, as soon as truth is drawn explicitly into the picture, it becomes at once evident that "truth in itself" is unintelligible. For truth always means unconcealedness and "unconcealedness in itself" does not offer any intelligible sense.

However, "being itself" likewise cannot be opposed to "being for man," for, if these two are distinguished in this fashion, "being itself" is necessarily regarded as "not for man." J. Lotz even goes so far as to present matters as if by means of "being itself" man could measure the truth of his thinking about "being for man."[123] His

---

[122] Luijpen, *Existential Phenomenology,* Pittsburgh, 4th impr., 1965, pp. 128 ff.

[123] "Weil das Denken . . . immer schon zu dem einen Selben des Seins durchstösst, ist es zuinnerst im *Ueberzeitlichen* beheimatet, an dem es die zeitlichen Abschattungen misst und von dem her es nicht jede von ihnen auf ihre Weise als echt wahr anerkennen kann. Damit kündigt sich das *Sein-an-sich* an . . .; darauf ist das Denken letztlich und erstlich bezogen, während es bei Heidegger letztlich und erstlich auf das Sein in der Sprache und als Sprache gerichtet ist." J. Lotz, "Denken und Sein nach den jüngsten Veröffentlichungen von M. Heidegger," *Scholastik,* vol. XXXIII (1958), p. 95.

position is perfectly identical with the claim of representative realism and, consequently, suffers from the same contradiction. Some scholastic philosophers vaguely are aware of the difficulty. They realize that the "being itself" that is contrasted with "being for man" would have to be "defined" as the non-affirmed and not-known being. They recognize that this being cannot be affirmed. However, they add, for the same reason it cannot be denied. "Being itself" can neither be affirmed nor denied.

If this position is taken, representative realism with its contradiction sneaks in again by the back door. Anyone who uses the term "being" as a "speaking word" (*parole parlante*), really affirms of something that it *is* and therefore affirms something. Consequently, he can no longer claim that he can neither affirm nor deny the being of that which he affirms, for he has already affirmed it. The realization that the "being" of representative realism would have to be "defined" as a non-affirmed being led Hume to skepticism. Considering his situation, we must say that he was right. Against the ideal of knowledge and truth defended by representative realism as an *absolute* postulate, one can only oppose skepticism. Scholastic philosophers, of course, do not accept skepticism. In its stead they defend the absolutism of truth, the absolute value of "truth in itself," and "forget" their "grasping" for truth. They admit that no one has a monopoly of the truth; nevertheless, Lotz evaluates the historical perspectives of truth with a "surveying glance," that is, he pretends to have an absolute "grip" on "truth in itself." He "forgets" his "grasping" for truth.

It is hardly necessary to point out that the essentialism, objectivism, or representationism of scholastic philosophy is a dangerous theory, for it can easily degenerate into an assault on man as a seeker for truth. Representationism does not lapse into skepticism, but elevates itself to absolutism, the absolutism of "truth in itself." "Truth in itself" is an absolute "light" for no one. Anyone can pretend to have it and, by virtue of this claim, regard as wrong anyone else who merely has "truth as a human possession" at his disposal. He then "piously kills his opponents."[124]

He "piously" kills them, says Merleau-Ponty. For the defense of "truth in itself" becomes, as it were, an act of piety as soon as "truth in itself" is represented as a participation in the Truth which God is. "Truth in itself" is regarded as being measured by its exemplars in God's intellect and is made real by a command of His divine will. Hence one who has "truth in itself" at his disposal looks at things from the "viewpoint" of God. He evaluates truth as a human possession by the standard of the truth of things for God. Who, then, would have the right to oppose his views? Only one who claims the right to disagree with God!

"To judge, I have only my own opinions at my disposal."[125] In the authentic search for, and affirmation of, truth there is no other truth than "truth as a human possession." This truth is based upon man's "grasping," with all the risks attached to that. The existent subject-as-*Cogito* himself is a "standing" in truth as unconcealedness, but this subject is not a pure *Cogito*. He is also a *Volo*, an "I will," and for this reason it can happen that he attaches all kinds of meanings to things, thinking that he "sees" these meanings. How many "visions" have not subsequently proved to be merely putative visions? How often does it not happen that man rejects an authentic vision, mistakenly thinking that it is merely a putative vision! All this is a necessary consequence of the fact that in his search for truth man has only "truth as a human

---

124 Merleau-Ponty, *Sens et Non-sens,* p. 190.

125 Ibid., p. 189.

possession" at his disposal. This truth cannot be measured with "truth in itself." Authentic thinking can never produce an "identity card"; it can never adduce anything lying outside the realm of thinking to give legitimacy to its results as being in agreement with reality.[126] There always remains a possibility of error.[127] Nevertheless, one would disregard its character by claiming that, on the basis of this possibility of error, authentic thinking is bound hand and foot to the subject's arbitrariness. The subject-as-*Cogito* is a "being responsive" to the call of being (*ein Wesen der Entsprechung*).[128]

The search for truth is marked by dizziness. Authentic thought recognizes this explicitly. The dizziness cannot be overcome but only disregarded. But to disregard it means to disregard the true character of thinking itself. One disregards it when one evaluates and measures man's "grasping" for truth by the standard of "truth in itself."[129]

Concluding, therefore, we may say that the essentialism of traditional scholasticism manifests the realism of the natural attitude. For this reason this trend of thinking displays, even in its most prominent representatives, "forgetfulness of being," in the sense which Heidegger gives to this expression. In the light of this conclusion, what possible value could still be attached to the reproach

---

[126] "Ich kann Ihnen, was Sie auch nicht verlangen, keine Ausweiskarte liefern, mit deren Hilfe das von mir Gesagte als mit 'der Wirklichkeit' übereinstimmend jederzeit bequem ausgewiesen werden könnte." Heidegger, *Vorträge und Aufsätze,* pp. 184-185.

[127] Heidegger, *ibid.,* p. 183.

[128] "Die Möglichkeit des Irrgangs ist bei diesem Denken die grösste. Dieses Denken kann sich nie ausweisen wie das mathematische Wissen. Aber es ist engensowenig Willkür, sondern gebunden an das Wesensgeschick des Seins." Heidegger, *ibid.,* p. 183.

[129] "Zu den seltsamen Erfahrungen, die ich mit meinem Vortrag mache, gehört auch die, dass man mein Denken danach befragt, woher es seine Weisung empfange, gleich als ob diese Frage nur gegenüber diesem Denken nötig sei." Heidegger, *ibid.,* p. 184.

that phenomenology cannot be a metaphysics since it cannot raise the question about be-ing as be-ing in the realistic sense, since consciousness of reality in phenomenology is not a consciousness of reality in the "strong," realistic sense of traditional metaphysics?

A Misinterpretation

It would be a mistake to interpret phenomenology's critique on the essentialism of traditional metaphysics in the sense that phenomenology:

> does not accept an idea of essence;
> does not strive for universal and necessary truth;
> does not acknowledge an aspect of immutability and eternity in man's knowledge;
> claims that knowledge does not have its norm in reality;
> rejects the idea that there is order;
> pretends that there are no ethically binding norms;
> asserts that the act of marriage is not essentially ordered to reproduction;
> states that God is not the source of all truth.

Any such interpretation of phenomenology is a mistake. Although that mistake has already been made, we cannot develop these points here, for we are now concerned only with realism. And with respect to realism, let us add that it would be a mistake also to think that phenomenology does not defend a realistic consciousness of reality because it rejects the representative realism of the natural attitude.

3. Phenomenological Realism

The Autonomy of Meaning as Term of Encounter

In defending the reality of the world, phenomenology rejects, on the one hand, that the world is a content of a subject-as-*Cogito* and, on the other, that the world is a "world in itself," in the sense given to this term by representative realism.[130] Man and knowledge, as a mode of being man, are "encounter," and for this reason we must reject any attempt to divorce subject and meaning from each other.[131] Both idealism and representative realism make such a divorce.

To express the reality of meaning as term of encounter, phenomenology uses the words "in itself," thereby indicating that meaning is not a content of the subject-as-*Cogito*. To distinguish the phenomenological "in itself" from the "in itself" of representative realism, phenomenology uses the words "for us." Meaning, therefore, as term of encounter, is an "in itself for us"; the being of meaning is a "being for us"; and the autonomy of being that is proper to meaning is an autonomy with respect to the subject.

For some opponents of phenomenology these statements alone are enough to raise reservations based on the suspicion that phenomenology could undermine realism. Let us give a few examples. According to Lotz,

> Heidegger is right when he describes only that which immediately manifests itself. The form of being which we encounter immediately depends indeed on man's mind, implies an orientation to this mind and does not constitute something standing as an opposite by itself. Nevertheless, Heidegger does not seem to stop there, for there are many signs that he denies a form of being which transcends what im-

---

[130] "La chose ne peut jamais être séparée de quelqu'un qui la perçoive, elle ne peut jamais être effectivement en soi, parce que ses articulations sont celles mêmes de notre existence et qu'elle se pose au bout d'un regard ou au terme d'une exploration sensorielle qui l'investit d'humanité." *Phénoménologie de la perception*, p. 370.

[131] "Le sens, en un mot, est essentiellement *rencontre*." De Waelhens, *op. cit.*, p. 81.

mediately manifests itself and which constitutes something that is in itself.[132]

Lotz is still hesitant in his formulation of the objection that phenomenology endangers the autonomy of being proper to meaning. M. Corvez, however, goes much farther when he calls meaning, as it is conceived by phenomenology, a phantom:

> The drama of Heidegger's philosophy is that he conceives being as an entity without consistency. Undoubtedly, this being lies beyond be-ing and is more profound than it in a certain sense; nevertheless, it is explicitly denied all density. Being comes to *Dasein*, who shapes it while receiving it, to the extent that it is only being in him. However, although being comes to, gives itself to, and is destined only for *Dasein*, it is only what *Dasein* sees. Being is this revelation itself: the presence of that which has being, which is being only to the extent that it appears. Such is the disgrace of Heideggerian phenomenology. It does not admit in being the dimension which would give it the depth of a genuine mystery. It does not give being any other light and truth than the light which illuminates me, to the extent that it illuminates me, and only to that extent. Must we not say that being is sterilized here, reduced to a phantom?[133]

D. de Petter also is convinced that phenomenology does not recognize the autonomy of being proper to meaning. Meaning, he holds, is entirely surrendered to the subject-as-*Cogito*, so that the latter practically acquires a creative value. As a consequence, the necessity to affirm God

---

[132] J. Lotz, "Denken und Sein nach den jüngsten Veröffentlichungen von M. Heidegger," *Scholastik,* vol. XXXIII (1958), p. 90.

[133] M. Corvez, "La place de Dieu dans l'ontologie de Martin Heidegger," *Revue Thomiste,* 1955, p. 381.

as Creator is completely eliminated; hence phenomenology is profoundly atheistic:

> The affirmation of God would become somehow superfluous if consciousness itself could be the foundation of be-ings.[134]

In the preceding pages we have drawn attention to the "forgetfulness of being" from which these critical remarks originate. Nevertheless, they acquire a semblance of correctness if they are regarded in the light of certain statements that constantly recur in phenomenology. For phenomenology claims that there *is* no world without the subject. A few pertinent quotations may serve to illustrate this point:

> If no *Dasein* exists, no world is "there" either.[135]

> There is being only as long as there is *Dasein*.[136]

> When *Dasein* does not exist, "independence" "is" not either, nor "is" the "in itself."[137]

> No thing "is" where the word, that is, a name is lacking. The word only gives the thing being.[138]

> Without man there are neither "things" nor "world" nor anything to which being can be attributed.[139]

> Without the subject or transcendence, there would be nothing.[140]

From these and other statements some people draw the conclusion that phenomenology does not recognize

134 De Petter, "Le caractère métaphysique de la preuve de l'existence de Dieu et la pensée contemporaine," *L'existence de Dieu*, p. 174.

135 *Sein und Zeit*, p. 365.

136 Heidegger, *Ueber den Humanismus*, p. 24.

137 *Sein und Zeit*, p. 212

138 Heidegger, *Unterwegs zur Sprache*, Pfullingen, 2nd ed., 1960, p. 164.

139 De Waelhens, *op. cit.*, p. 175.

140 De Waelhens, *ibid.*, p. 186.

the autonomy of being proper to meaning and consequently does not defend an authentic consciousness of reality. For, phenomenology claims not only that without man (rather without the subject) no world can be affirmed, but also that without man there *is* no world, not merely no world for man but simply no world at all.[141] While its claim that without the subject no world can be affirmed must be admitted in order to avoid lapsing into representative realism, the statement that without the subject there is no world implies, they say, relativism and atheism.[142] Phenomenology asserts not only that the world with which man deals is a world for man, but also that there *is* only a world for man and that without man there can be no world.[143] This, so these metaphysicians add, is the denial of the authentic consciousness of reality and of realism.[144]

We could dispose of this objection by pointing out that anyone who claims that there *is* a world without man can *really* make this claim only by *de facto* not making the supposition that there is no man. For he presupposes his own subjectivity-as-*Cogito*,[145] and this subjectivity, as the "letting be" of meaning, constitutes meaning as autonomy of being with respect to the subject, an autonomy which is the norm of every statement. Real statements,

---

[141] De Petter, "Een geamendeerde phenomenologie," *Tijdschrift voor Philosophie,* vol. XXII (1960), p. 292.

[142] E. Schillebeeckx, "De natuurwet in verband met de katholieke huwelijksopvatting," *Jaarboek van het werkgenootschap van katholieke theologen in Nederland,* 1961, p. 6.

[143] De Petter, *Metaphysiek en phenomenologie,* p. 4.

[144] De Petter, *op. cit.* (footnote 141), *passim;* Plat, *op. cit., passim.*

[145] "Le noyau de toute position phénoménologique, l'irréductible de toute réduction, l'aboutissement du chemin qui mène vers 'les choses elles-mêmes' est cette aperception dernière et invincible: le sens surgit avec l'homme." De Waelhens, *op. cit.,* p. 98.

that is, statements about reality, always presuppose the subject who as *Cogito* is involved in reality and this *Cogito* can never be thought really away. The existent subject-as-*Cogito* is the implicit "affirmation" of the autonomy of being with respect to the subject, to which every explicit affirmation refers and which is presupposed in every explicit affirmation. One who thinks away this implicit "affirmation" can no longer really speak, but only manipulate the "spoken word" (*parole parlée*).[146] He can use the words: "Without man there *is* a world," but he does not really want to affirm anything. Real affirmations presuppose the subject, and that is precisely what he has thought away. All that is left then is "talk."

This simple answer, however, can be made more profound by a reflection upon the sense of the "spoken word." We will do this in the following pages.

The Existent Subject-as-Cogito and the Word

Phenomenology adamantly refuses to divorce subject and meaning. Any attempt to separate these two means a relapse into the natural attitude, in which a defense of realism is necessarily a defense of representative realism. One who asserts that meaning *is* without the subject, who distinguishes the world-for-man from the world "itself," or opposes "truth as a human possession" to "truth in itself" cannot escape from speaking surreptitiously, in spite of everything, about meaning-for-the-subject, from representing the world as a world-for-the-subject, and from affirming "truth in itself" as a human possession. He inevitably falls into contradictions.[147] However, he does not realize these contradictions because he does not realize that this meaning without the subject is

146 *Phénoménologie de la perception*, p. 229.

147 "Il est impossible aussi de parler d'une 'vérité des choses' constituée hors de nous." De Waelhens, *op. cit.*, p. 35.

de facto a meaning whose moment of "letting be" by the subject is "forgotten." He does not realize that his meaning without a subject is the meaning whose never-finished, personal and collective history of dis-closure he regards as finished, that it is a meaning which is torn loose from its mooring in the encounter. Ultimately he no longer realizes that such a "meaning" can no longer be really be spoken of. In Heidegger's words, he "forgets" even his "forgetfulness of being."[148]

These are the reasons why phenomenology demands that the philosopher abandon the natural attitude and perform the phenomenological reduction. For the same reasons, in Heideggerian terms, "representative" thinking must be replaced by authentic thinking, and, for the same reasons again, the "spoken word" must be replaced by the "speaking word."

Authentic thinking is equiprimordially the "speaking word." We have already characterized authentic thinking as an "event" of being and *Dasein* as the "place" where being "occurs" or rather, where the "event" of truth of being comes to be through the subject's thinking. The truth of being is the unconcealedness of meaning, and meaning is unconcealed through the never-finished history of the "letting be" which *Dasein* as natural light itself is. In other words, the subject-as-*Cogito* refers to the meaning, and the meaning refers to the subject-as-*Cogito*. The unity of reciprocal implication of subject and meaning *is* the coming to be, the occurrence, of truth, and this occurrence is equiprimordially speech, language.

---

148 "Denken wir jedoch die Seinsfrage im Sinne der Frage nach dem Sein als solchem, dann wird jedem Mitdenkenden klar, dass der Metaphysik das Sein *als solches* gerade verborgen, in der Vergessenheit bleibt und dies so entschieden, dass die Vergessenheit des Seins, die selber in die Vergessenheit fällt, der unbekannte, aber ständige Anstoss für das metaphysische Fragen ist." Heidegger, *Einführung in die Metaphysik,* p. 15.

To understand this statement, it is indispensable that language be viewed as more than an instrument for information and communication[149] which transfers thoughts, "finished" in the "interiority" of the subject-as-*Cogito* and destined for others, to man's "exteriority." The subject-as-*Cogito* is an embodied subject, which implies that there is no thought without the word. Man's thinking takes place and comes to fullness in and through the word.[150] One who cannot say what he is thinking, does not yet really think; one who wants to achieve intellectual mastery over a problem should try to write a book about it or prepare to lecture about it in a university.[151] There exists no separation between the "interiority" of thinking and the "exteriority" of the world, but rather a unity of reciprocal implication. The word is permeated with the "light" of the subject-as-*Cogito*, and the subject-as-*Cogito* is a "light" only in and through the word. To speak is more than to contract the throat or to move the larynx while expelling air between the tongue and the teeth.[152]

The existent subject-as-*Cogito* is the "letting be" of meaning, the bringing about of truth as the unconcealedness of meaning. Because the *Cogito* is equiprimordially speech, we must say that speaking lets meaning be, that speaking brings about the truth of meaning.[153] In the

---

[149] "Wir . . . suchen die unzerstörte Nennkraft der Sprache und Worte wieder zu erobern; denn die Worte und Sprache sind keine Hülsen, worin die Dinge nur für den redenden und schreibenden Verkehr verpackt werden." Heidegger, *ibid.*, p. 11.

[150] "La pensée tend vers l'expression comme vers son achèvement." *Phénoménologie de la perception*, p. 206.

[151] *Ibid.*, p. 206.

[152] *Ibid.*, p. 226.

[153] "Indem die Sprache erstmals das Seiende nennt, bringt solches Nennen das Seiende erst zum Wort und zum Erscheinen. Dieses Nennen ernennt das Seiende erst zu seinem Sein aus diesem.

word the subject lives and dwells in the meaning, through the word the meaning is called forth and appeals to the subject.[154] There is no meaning without the word, and there is no world without language.[155] "Speech is the dwelling of being."[156]

Accordingly, speech is the primordial "occurrence" of meaning, of truth, of unconcealedness. Where there is no speech there is no meaning, no truth, no unconcealedness, there is nothing that appeals to man.[157] But the fact that there is something that appeals to man means that man is man. Speech, therefore, constitutes the essence of being-man.[158] Without language, man would not be what he is, without language, meaning would not be what it is. Speaking brings about the essence of man[159] and makes meaning be meaning. The speaking subject and meaning belong inseparably together, they constitute a unity of reciprocal implication.[160] In his speaking man is, of course, not the master of meaning but merely its shepherd, for authentic speaking is equiprimordially a listening and a being docile.[161]

Solches Sagen ist ein Entwerden des Lichten, darin angesagt wird, als was das Seiende ins Offene kommt." Heidegger, *Holzwege,* p. 60-61.

[154] "Im Wort, in der Sprache werden und sind erst die Dinge." Heidegger, *ibid.,* p. 11.

[155] "Etwas *ist* nur, wo das geeignete und also zuständige Wort etwas als seiend nennt und so das jeweilige Seiende als solches stiftet." Heidegger, *Unterwegs zur Sprache,* Pfullingen, 2nd ed., 1960, p. 165.

[156] Heidegger, *ibid.,* p. 166.

[157] "Wo keine Sprache west . . . da ist auch keine Offenheit des Seienden." Heidegger, *Holzwege,* p. 60.

[158] Heidegger, *Unterwegs zur Sprache,* p. 11.

[159] Heidegger, *ibid.,* p. 241.

[160] "Ohne das also verhaltende Wort sinkt das Ganze der Dinge, die 'Welt' ins Dunkel weg, samt dem 'Ich'." Heidegger, *ibid.,* p. 177.

[161] Heidegger, *ibid.,* p. 255.

These remarks obviously refer to authentic speech, they try to explicitate the "speaking word," which is much more than a manipulating of terms. They refer to primordial speech, the kind of speaking which really says something because, as embodiment of dwelling thinkingly in meaning, it tries to give voice to the reality of meaning. The dwelling of the subject-as-*Cogito* in meaning is always an implicit "affirmation" of the reality of meaning. The word is the embodiment of the existent subject-as-*Cogito*, it is a really speaking word when it is animated by the "affirmation" which the subject-as-*Cogito* himself is. Without the subject's implicit "affirmation," the word is an empty dwelling, something which the "speaker" can manipulate in a purely verbal fashion. If he does this, he does not really say anything.[162]

It should be evident now why the phenomenologist does not hesitate to say that without the subject there is no world. His statement is based on the consideration that the term "is" has meaning and really says something only in an affirmation. In the affirmation being manifests itself as being-present, as being-for-the-subject. If, then, he claims that without the subject there *is* no world, he asserts that without the subject there is no world-for-the-subject. Such an assertion may "sound" trivial, and the statement that without man there is no world "sounds" nonsensical. Words, however, are not "sounds," but refer to meaning. Their meaning can be understood only by one who really tries to speak with his fellow-men.

Phenomenology is sometimes accused of making exactly the same mistake as it attributes to the adherents

---

[162] "Sagen und Sprechen sind nicht das gleiche. Einer kann sprechen, spricht endlos, und alles ist nichtssagend . . . Doch was heisst sagen ? Um dies zu erfahren, sind wir an das gehalten, was unsere Sprache selber uns bei diesem Wort zu denken heisst. 'Sagen' heisst: zeigen, erscheinen-, sehen-, und hören-lassen." Heidegger, *ibid.*, p. 252.

of representative realism. These accusers admit that it is nonsense to claim that there is a world without the subject because such a claim evidently presupposes the subject. However, they add, for exactly the same reason it is nonsense to claim that without the subject there is no world since this negation cannot be really made if the subject is thought away.

In a certain sense this objection is valid. If phenomenology really intended to make a denial without a subject, this denial would be in contradiction with the supposition that there is no subject. However, the intention of this negative statement is positively to affirm the unity of reciprocal implication of subject and meaning as the authentic and only possible dimension in which there can be *real* thinking and speaking.

If attention is paid to what is intended by certain statements rather than to the way this intention is expressed, phenomenology is not unwilling to agree with certain assertions which it itself does not make in that form. For instance, in order to ascertain that phenomenology does not destroy the autonomy of being proper to meaning, someone may demand that it admit the existence of trees and fishes even if all human beings are dead,[163] or that there were geological eras before there were geologists.[164] In such a case phenomenology sees no difficulty in making these admissions with respect to those who otherwise accept that the authentic and only possible dimension of real thinking and speaking is found in the unity of the reciprocal implication of subject and meaning. The condition remains, however, that those statements do not intend to affirm anything else than the autonomy of being proper to meaning with respect to the subject.

---

[163] J. Plat, *Traditionele metafysiek en fenomenologie,* p. 13.

[164] H. Geurtsen, "Fenomenologie en atheisme, Kritische studie," *Bijdragen,* 1963, pp. 308-309.

Accordingly, phenomenology does not undermine the autonomy of being proper to meaning and it does not deny that meaning manifests itself as "independent." It is, therefore, a realistic philosophy. However, phenomenology refuses to cast meaning as an "in itself" outside the encounter or to manipulate words as if they were empty shells. The "back to the things themselves" or the phenomenological reduction, therefore, is equiprimordially a return to the "speaking word."

Phenomenology and Metaphysics

Metaphysics tries to explicitate what it means that man says of anything whatsoever that it *is*. Metaphysics speaks therefore about "everything." However, it is not "a tale told by an idiot," for it inquires into "everything" from a "special" standpoint. It speaks about be-ing *as* be-ing, about meaning *as* meaning, about the "universe" as the universality of be-ing as be-ing.

Here lies the inspiration of scholastic metaphysical thinking. This inspiration is authentic and cannot be rejected without being presupposed in its very negation because "standing in the universe" is something that "occurs" in *Dasein* itself. Nevertheless, in its development of its inspiration, traditional metaphysics assumes the natural attitude and presupposes representative realism—to such an extent that almost everyone thinks that asking about be-ing as be-ing equals denying intentionality and the phenomenological reduction, forgetting the origin of metaphysics, and letting the "speaking word" degenerate into "talk."

Accordingly, the metaphysical question must be "brought home" again, and its repeating must include a return to the ground, the source from which it springs.[165]

---

[165] "Fragen: Wie steht es um das Sein ? - das besagt Geringeres als den Anfang unseres geschichtlich-geistigen Daseins *wieder-holen,*

It is necessary therefore to apply the phenomenological reduction and to return to the intentional subject as "speaking word." Then the subject will be able to appear again as the bringing about of the truth of the "universe" as unconcealedness.[166] The "forgetfulness of being" will be overcome, and metaphysics will develop as a phenomenological metaphysics.

---

um ihn in den anderen Anfang zu verwandeln. Solches ist möglich . . . Ein Anfang wird aber nicht wiederholt, indem man sich auf ihn als ein Vormaliges und nunmehr Bekanntes und lediglich Nachzumachendes zurückschraubt, sondern indem der Anfang *ursprünglicher* wiederangefangen wird und zwar mit all dem Befremdlichen, Dunklen, Ungesicherten, das ein wahrhafter Anfang bei sich führt. Wiederholung . . . ist alles andere, nur nicht die verbessernde Weiterführung des Bisherigen mit den Mitteln des Bisherigen." Heidegger, *Einführung in die Metaphysik,* pp. 29-30.

[166] "Am Ende bestecht ein wesenhafter Unterschied zwischen dem Erfassen des Ganzen des Seienden an sich und dem Sichbefinden inmitten des Seienden im Ganzen. Jenes ist grundsätzlich unmöglich. Dieses geschieht ständig in unserem Dasein." Heidegger, *Was ist Metaphysik ?,* p. 30.

CHAPTER FOUR

PHENOMENOLOGY AND METAPHYSICS
IN ITS SECOND PHASE

1. *Introductory Remarks*

Traditional metaphysics reaches its apex in the affirmation of the Absolute, of that which explains everything and itself does not need to be explained. No matter how this Absolute is conceived, its affirmation always functions as a kind of ultimate anchor and as a terminus of man's thinking because beyond the Absolute it is not possible to raise any meaningful question. In the affirmation of the Absolute metaphysics unfolds itself as "radical" thinking in the full sense of the term. This radicalism is not merely a matter of encompassing the realm of metaphysics in "breadth," but rather of penetrating into its depth. For, metaphysics seeks to find a ground constituting the basis of anything of which, no matter how, man says that it *is*. Precisely in this respect thinking finds a kind of terminus, a point of rest, in the affirmation of the Absolute.

As we have mentioned, many phenomenologists reject the Absolute in the above-described sense because they want to safeguard the "metaphysical" in man. The rejection of the Absolute, they argue, is absolutely necessary for this purpose. Thus it appears that phenomenology itself supplies scholastic metaphysicians with a new argument in favor of their claim that phenomenology neither is nor can be a metaphysics. The phenomenologists themselves say it. The metaphysics of which there is question here is what we have called above "metaphysics in its second phase." Without the affirmation of the Absolute, metaphysics, at least in its second phase of development, is not what it ought to be.

With respect to metaphysics in its first phase, the reply to the question whether phenomenology is a metaphysics depends, as we have seen, on the sense attached to the term "realism." For the second phase the crucial question is what exactly is meant by the term "the Absolute." Just as it can happen that one defends a false realism, so also can it happen that one has a false notion of the Absolute. The fact that phenomenology rejects the Absolute in the strict sense could mean that phenomenology rejects false notions about this Absolute.

To throw a modicum of light on this issue, it will be necessary to investigate, first of all, whether phenomenology is essentially in conflict with the inspiration of metaphysics in the second stage of its development. Next, we must see what is meant by the "metaphysical" for the sake of which the Absolute is rejected. Finally, we must establish what the Absolute represents in the eyes of those who think that this Absolute asphyxiates the "metaphysical" in man and determine whether they are right in their conception of the Absolute.

2. *Phenomenology and the Inspiration of Metaphysics in Its Second Phase*

Why is There Something Rather Than Nothing?

In the preceding pages we have defended the legitimacy and even the inevitability of the question about something as something, about be-ing as be-ing, about meaning as meaning. With respect to something, as opposed to nothing, however, traditional metaphysics inquires into the "why," and the necessity of asking this question is interpreted as the necessity of asking about the cause of be-ing as be-ing.

Heidegger has voiced objections against this way of asking the metaphysical question.[1] For, precisely by seeking at once to find the cause of be-ing as be-ing, metaphysics became blind for the wonder of the appearing of be-ing. It simply took be-ing for granted and acted as if the appearing of be-ing did not give rise to any question. As a consequence metaphysics fell under the spell of thinking in the natural attitude and became "forgetful of being."

According to Heidegger, the question regarding the "why" of be-ing had an entirely different sense in ancient Greece. The old Greeks still understood "reality" (*das Wirkliche*) in its original sense. Playing on the etymology of the German language, Heidegger says: "*Das Wirkliche ist das Wirkende, Gewirkte.*"[2] By substituting "actual" for his *wirklich* and understanding that term as if it meant "real," we could approximately transliterate his words by saying: "The 'actual' is that which 'acts' (works) or that which has been brought out by 'acting'." According to Heidegger, the "real" (*das Wirkliche*) was understood by the old Greeks as that which has been "brought to presence."[3] The term *werken*, to act or to

---

[1] "Insofern diese Frage (nach dem Seienden) gar noch in der herkömmlichen Weise der Metaphysik am Leitfaden des Warum ? kausal fragt, wird das Denken an das Sein zugunsten der vorstellenden Erkenntnis von Seiendem aus Seiendem völlig verleugnet." Heidegger, *Was ist Metaphysik ?*, p. 22.

[2] Heidegger, *Vorträge und Aufsätze*, p. 49.

[3] " 'Wirklichkeit' meint dann, weit genug gedacht: das ins Anwesen hervor-gebrachte Vorliegen, das in sich vollendete Anwesen von Sichhervorbringendem." Heidegger, *ibid.*, p. 49.

work, did not express to produce an effect but the fact that something is pro-duced, brought forward, and comes to stand in unconcealedness.[4] When the Greeks spoke of what the Latins would later call an "efficient cause," they never meant to refer to the production of an effect.[5] They spoke of *energeia*, but this term, which is derived from *ergon*, work, did not have the same content as our energy in reference to a producing cause. The Greek *energeia*, says Heidegger, meant "presence" (*Anwesen*), and the latter may be translated by "reality" (*Wirklichkeit*) only when *ergon*, work, is understood as the old Greeks understood it, viz., as to pro-duce, to "bring out," to "bring into unconcealedness," to "bring forward," to "bring to presence" (" '*her'—ins Unverborgene, 'vor'—ins Anwesen bringen*").[6] What follows from "working" is that which has been wrought, the **"real"** (*das Wirkliche*), conceived not as the product of an efficient cause, but as that which has come forward from concealedness, the "present," the meaning as "in itself for us."[7] Because metaphysics no longer understood the "real" (*das Wirkliche*) as that which is pro-duced, brought from concealedness, but regarded it as that which is produced, the effect, it disregarded all questions concerning the unconcealedness of reality and began at once to search for the cause. Thus it resigned itself to the "forgetfulness of being" proper to the natural attitude.

---

[4] Heidegger, *ibid.*, p. 49.

[5] Heidegger, *ibid.*, pp. 49-50.

[6] Heidegger, *ibid.*, p. 50.

[7] "Das Her- und Vor-gebrachte erscheint jetzt als das, was sich aus einer operatio er-gibt. Das Ergebnis ist das, was aus einer und auf in actio folgt: der Er-folg. Das Wirkliche ist jetzt das Er-folgte. Der Erfolg wird durch eine Sache erbracht, die ihm vor-aufgeht, durch die Ursache (causa). Das Wirkliche erscheint jetzt im Lichte der Kausalität der causa efficiens." Heidegger, *ibid.*, p. 50.

To overcome the natural attitude, Heidegger, as we have seen, wants metaphysics to return to its ground, to take the "step back" to its essence. By this "return of thinking" traditional metaphysics is transcended.[8] Metaphysics overcomes the natural attitude and, by making the phenomenological reduction, it recovers its authentic dimension.

Let us add at once that Heidegger's attention is almost exclusively concentrated upon the description of the dimension proper to authentic questioning and thinking. The description of the character proper to authentic questioning ("the 'piety' of thinking"[9]) and to authentic thinking as modes of *Dasein's* being,[10] undoubtedly means much more for Heidegger than a reflection upon the *content* of the question concerning the "why" of be-ing as be-ing, much more also than a reply to this question. Without any sign that it may be necessary to make certain differentiations, Heidegger accuses traditional metaphysics unqualifiedly of having interpreted the question of the "why" of be-ing as an inquiry into the cause of be-ing.[11]

---

8 "Diese Kehre ist nicht eine Änderung des Standpunktes von 'Sein und Zeit' zu 'Zeit und Sein', sondern in ihr gelangt das versuchte Denken erst in die Ortschaft der Dimension, aus der 'Sein und Zeit' erfahren ist und zwar erfahren aus der Grunderfahrung der Seinsvergessenheit." Heidegger. *Ueber den Humanismus,* p. 17.

9 Heidegger, *Vorträge und Aufsätze,* p. 44.

10 "Seinsverständnis besagt, dass der Mensch seinem Wesen nach im Offenen des Entwurfs des Seins steht . . . Nur insofern der Mensch seinem Wesen nach in einer Lichtung des Seins steht, ist er ein denkendes Wesen." Heidegger, *Der Satz vom Grund,* pp. 146-147.

11 "Das Gesagte des Satzes gelangt ins Selbstverständliche: 'Seiendes ist'. Was soll das Seiende anderes als 'sein', wenn es schon ist ? Man möchte jetzt nur noch wissen, *warum* Seiendes ist. Man fragt daher: wodurch wird Seiendes bewirkt ? Denn es ist doch das Wirkliche und als solches bewirkt und wirkend und überall auf Ursachen bezogen." Heidegger, *Was heisst Denken ?,* p. 167.

Thus he represents matters as if it is unqualifiedly excluded that man's thinking could ever arrive at a phase in which the question of the "why" would have to be interpreted as referring to the cause even in metaphysics. Yet, we must ask, is it really so certain that this possibility is unqualifiedly excluded?

For traditional metaphysicians the search for the "why" of be-ing refers solely to the cause of be-ing, but for Heidegger it does not at all refer to that cause. For him the question means to search for a ground which makes this question itself possible.[12] This is not surprising, for Heidegger was one of the first philosophers to realize the impossible situation in which metaphysics had become entangled and the necessity of overcoming the natural attitude. For this reason Max Müller is right when he says that many Thomists in their hurry miss Heidegger's main concern by giving the Thomistic reply to his question of being.[13] The Thomistic answer is a reply to a question of being but not to Heidegger's question of being. Heidegger's question is concerned with the unconcealedness of meaning. Neo-scholastic philosophy does not touch this question, and for this reason it remains in the natural attitude. In other words, one who unqualifiedly presents neo-scholastic thinking as *the* answer to Heidegger's questions fails to come to grips with his concern and remains stuck in the natural attitude.

However, such a conclusion does not cover all the aspects of the problem. If Heidegger's question about the "why" of be-ing demands that metaphysics take a "step back" and return to the "source" of metaphysical think-

---

[12] "Darnach besagt Begründung soviel wie Ermöglichung der Warumfrage überhaupt." Heidegger, *Vom Wesen des Grundes,* p.

[13] M. Müller, *Existenzphilosophie im geistigen Leben der Gegenwart,* p. 113.

ing which lies in the being of *Dasein*,[14] then the first reply to the question, "Why is there something rather than nothing?" is: "Because there is *Dasein*, which as existential thinking co-constitutes truth as the unconcealedness of being."[15] Through this answer Heidegger takes the "step back" from traditional metaphysics to the ground, the origin, the essence of metaphysics. This return implies abandoning the natural attitude and making the phenomenological reduction. Man's thinking is thus placed on its authentic, existential ground, which is found in the unity of reciprocal implication of subject and meaning.

The question, however, is whether, after making the phenomenological reduction, we must not again ask: "Why is there something rather than nothing?", in a new and more profound sense. Is it not necessary to ask about the "cause" of be-ing as be-ing? Can the affirmation of meaning, understood as the autonomy of being proper to meaning with respect to the subject, be safeguarded if the subject does not do anything else but affirm the meaning?

With these questions we penetrate into the authentic inspiration of traditional metaphysics in its second phase. After the phenomenological reduction is made, the question of the "why" of be-ing does indeed return in the form

---

[14] "Das Hinausgehen über das Seiende geschieht im Wesen des Daseins. Dieses Hinausgehen aber ist die Metaphysik selbst. Darin liegt: Die Metapsysik gehört zur 'Natur des Menschen' . . . Die Metaphysik ist das Grundgeschehen im Dasein. Sie ist das Dasein selbst." Heidegger, *Was ist Metaphysik ?*, p. 41.

[15] "Zum Wesen des Seins aber gehört Grund, weil es Sein (nicht Seiendes) nur gibt in der Transzendenz als dem weltentwerfend befindlichen Gründen. So dann ist bezüglich des Satzes vom Grunde deutlich geworden, dass der 'Geburtsort' dieses Prinzips weder im Wesen der Aussage noch in der Aussagewahrheit, sondern in der ontologischen Wahrheit, d.h. aber in der Transzendenz selbst liegt. *Die Freiheit ist der Ursprung des Satzes vom Grunde;* denn in ihr, der Einheit von Ueberschwung und Entzug, gründet sich das als ontologische Wahrheit sich ausbildende Begründen." Heidegger, *Vom Wesen des Grundes,* p. 51.

of an inquiry into the cause of be-ing as be-ing. For, be-ing manifests itself as wholly contingent, and this means that metaphysical thinking reaches a phase in which it is no longer possible to affirm that be-ing *is*. Be-ing simply *cannot* be if there "is" nothing else but be-ings.[16] The subject, as "shepherd of being," cannot do otherwise than "tend," i.e., recognize, the complete groundlessness of be-ing. As soon, however, as the subject recognizes this groundlessness, the question of "why" arises again. For, whatever is without a ground in itself, whatever is not "from itself" and nonetheless *is*, is "from something else." The being of a be-ing is a being from something else than be-ing. This "being from something else" is traditionally called "being caused."

However, the term "cause" should not be misunderstood. It suffers under a hereditary burden because it has too often been taken in the sense in which the degeneration of the sciences known as "scientism" wants to use it. In this sense the term is useless in metaphysics. Metaphysical thinking is concerned with the universe of be-ings and not with the particular fields of meaning which the questioning attitude of the special sciences draw into the center of attention of the existent subject-as-*Cogito*. The fact that metaphysics does not use the term "cause" in the same sense as any of the special sciences does not allow anyone to conclude that therefore this term is meaningless in metaphysics.

The realization that the being of a be-ing is a "being from something else than be-ing" calls immediately for the question about the "other than be-ing" as cause of be-ing. One who does not raise this question stops midway in his thinking and does not think radically.

---

[16] For the stages through which the metaphysical consciousness develops see Luijpen, *Phenomenology and Atheism,* pp. 70 ff.

Neo-scholastic philosophers, therefore, are right when they claim that Heidegger has not reached this radical stage.[17] He is so absorbed in the "step back" to the source of metaphysics, in establishing the authentic dimension of thinking, that he does not arrive at radicalism as it is conceived by traditional metaphysics and as it has to be conceived. This statement does not mean, of course, that metaphysics, in order to reach the radicalism proper to the inspiration of its thinking must again lapse into the natural attitude and its accompanying representative realism. The metaphysical question about be-ing as be-ing is the question about meaning as meaning. Nevertheless, one who returns to the ground of metaphysics and therefore makes the phenomenological reduction is not entitled to omit subsequently this authentically metaphysical question. The existent-subject-as-*Cogito* himself, as "functioning intentionality," is the always active recognition and affirmation of meaning as autonomy of being. This autonomy of being, however, reveals itself as "being from something else"; hence the existent subject-as *Cogito* is, equiprimordially with being the always active recognition and affirmation of be-ing, also *implicitly* the "recognition" and the "affirmation" of the "other than be-ing." This implicit "recognition" and "affirmation" are unfolded by metaphysics in its second phase.

The Metaphysical "Affirmation" of God

The question that arises next is how the "other than be-ing," the cause of be-ing, should be called.

In scholastic metaphysics the cause of be-ing is called "God." Others raise serious objections against this scho-

---

17 "Heidegger's concern continues to be the ground of the appearing of be-ings and not the ground on which be-ings have autonomy of being." De Petter, *Metaphysiek en phaenomenologie,* p. 5.

lastic tradition. In spite of their respectable nature, these objections imply a misconception regarding the intention of those who identify the Cause of be-ing with God. What kind of a God is this?, they ask. And replying to their own question, they add: Certainly not a God to whom man can pray, offer a sacrifice, for whom he can fall on his knees, play music or dance. One who rejects the Cause-God is closer to the true God than the one who affirms this Cause-God.[18]

These objectors, however, are mistaken if they think that those who call the Cause of be-ing "God" have the intention to affirm that man can pray to the Cause of be-ing, that he can offer a sacrifice to this Cause, fall on his knees, play music or dance before this Cause of be-ing. The objectors have in mind the personal God of Christian revelation and cannot bear the idea that metaphysics says anything whatsoever about this God. It is evident, of course, that metaphysics cannot express all the wealth contained in the Christian revelation of God. It would be ridiculous to assume that surreptitiously it nonetheless wants to do that. On the other hand, it is also undeniable that in Christian revelation God is also called unqualifiedly the Cause, the Origin, the Creator of everything. This, precisely, is something that metaphysics can "affirm." In this sense it is undeniable that metaphysics says *something* about God—so much that it is no longer an irrational "leap" for man as a rational be-ing to enter the realm of revelation. Only after his entrance there

---

[18] "Dies ist die Ursache als die Causa sui. So lautet der sachgerechte Name für den Gott in der Philosophie. Zu diesem Gott kann der Mensch weder beten, noch kann er ihm opfern. Vor der Causa sui kann der Mensch weder aus Scheu ins Knie fallen, noch kann er vor diesem Gott musizieren und tanzen. Demgemäss ist das gott-lose Denken, das den Gott der Philosophie, den Gott als Causa sui preisgeben muss, dem göttlichen Gott vielleicht näher. Dies sagt hier nur: Es ist freier für ihn, als es die Onto-Theo-Logik wahrhaben möchte." Heidegger, *Identität und Differenz*, p. 70-71.

can he fall on his knees, pray to God and play music for Him.

The Onto-theo-logical Conception of Metaphysics

Our defense of the claim that metaphysics does tell us something when it "affirms" God as the Origin, Cause and Creator of everything is not wholly without reservation. For there exists a way of thinking about God as Cause which really forces the thinker to reject "God" as Cause. The rejection of that way of thinking does not eliminate God but brings man closer to Him.

This bad way of thinking about "God" as Cause is what Heidegger had in mind when he wrote the above-mentioned objection to the causal God. For this reason we will try here to penetrate somewhat more profoundly into the scope of Heidegger's objection, for he accuses traditional metaphysics in its second phase of thinking in a faulty fashion.

Since its start in ancient Greece, Heidegger says, metaphysics has always developed in two phases.[19] On the one hand, it reflected upon be-ing as be-ing or be-ing in general. As such it was an ontology. On the other hand, metaphysics spoke about be-ing in its supreme realization, about be-ing not in general but in its apex, the divine be-ing.[20] As such metaphysics is theology. The "first philosophy," therefore, as ontology is at the same time

---

[19] "Aber die Metaphysik stellt die Seiendheit des Seienden in zweifacher Weise vor: einmal das Ganze des Seienden als solchen im Sinne seiner allgemeinsten Züge (*on katholon, koinon*); zugleich aber das Ganze des Seienden als solchen im Sinne des höchsten und darum göttlichen Seienden (*on katholon, akrotaton, Theion*)." Heidegger, *Was ist Metaphysik?*, p. 19.

[20] "Die Metaphysik ist in sich, und zwar weil sie das Seiende als das Seiende zur Vorstellung bringt, zweifach-einig die Wahrheit des Seienden im Allgemeinen und im Höchsten. Sie ist ihrem Wesen nach zugleich Ontologie im engeren Sinne und Theologie." Heidegger, *ibid.*, p. 19.

143

also a theology of the supreme be-ing. In an incredibly confusing and ambiguous way, however, this supreme be-ing is also called "Being" itself.[21]

According to Heidegger, ontology and theology were conceived in the same way as psychology, biology, cosmology and archeology;[22] in other words, as sciences. As a "-logy" onto-theology displayed not only the logical element of internal coherence proper to any science but, like the sciences, endeavored to find the ground, the cause, of its topic, viz., be-ing as be-ing.[23] The highest be-ing was conceived by it as the "First Cause."[24] It was not surprising that it did this, Heidegger adds. For in metaphysics the actuality of be-ing is conceived as causality since every cause exercises its influence by virtue of its actuality. The highest be-ing, God, is highest precisely because it is pure actuality. It contains no potentiality whatsoever, but is pure act. Consequently, the highest be-ing is also supremely cause.[25]

When we spoke of the phenomenological reduction and opposed it to the natural attitude, we stressed that the latter is characterized by a two-fold conviction, viz.,

---

[21] "Dieses Seiende, *to Theion,* das Göttliche, wird in einer seltsamen Zweideutigkeit auch 'das Sein' genannt." Heidegger, *Holtzwege,* p. 179.

[22] Heidegger, *Identität und Differenz,* p. 55.

[23] *Ibid.,* pp. 56-57.

[24] "Die ursprüngliche Sache des Denkens stellt sich als die Ursache dar, als die causa prima, die dem begründenden Rückgang auf die ultima ratio, die letzte Rechenschaft, entspricht." Heidegger, *ibid.,* p. 57.

[25] "Die actualitas aber ist causalitas. Der Ursachecharakter des Seins als Wirklichkeit zeigt sich in aller Reinheit an jenem Seienden, das im höchsten Sinne das Wesen des Seins erfüllt, da es das Seiende ist, das nie nicht sein kann! 'Theologisch' gedacht, heisst dieses Seiende 'Gott' . . . Das höchste Seiende ist reine, stets erfüllte Verwirklichung, actus purus." Heidegger, *Nietzsche,* vol. II, p. 415.

knowledge is a mirroring of the "in itself" and *the* system of objective mirroring is the system of the sciences. In other words, the natural attitude adheres to representative realism and to scientism. For Heidegger this means forgetfulness of being and nihilism. These are overcome by the "step back" of metaphysics to its essence and this "step back" is identical with that of technology to its essence. Heidegger, then, wants to say, so it seems, that traditional metaphysics is infected by the scientism of our technocratic order. The forgetfulness of being and nihilism of both metaphysics and technocracy are transcended by replacing their "representative" thinking by authentic thinking.

All this throws some light on the way in which Heidegger conceives the search of traditional metaphysics for the First Cause. In his eyes, metaphysics wanted to be a "science" in order to be able to defend itself against the sciences;[26] hence its search for the First Cause was, for Heidegger, a search for a cause which within the series of causes discovered by the sciences, should be regarded as first.[27] The First Cause spoken of by metaphysics, according to Heidegger, does not differ essentially from the causes occurring within the chain of scientific causes; yet traditional metaphysics called that cause "God." This "God," whom Heidegger calls the "God of philosophy," must be rejected. However, when man's thinking becomes godless by this rejection, it is not atheistic.[28] It is closer to the "divine God" than is traditional metaphysics. For, making the phenomenological reduction is a first requirement for placing man's thinking in the dimension in

---

26 Heidegger, *Ueber den Humanismus*, p. 6.

27 "Der Grund verlangt, überall so zum Vorschein zu kommen, dass alles . . . als eine Folge erscheint und d.h. als Konsequenz vorgestellt werden muss." Heidegger, *Der Satz vom Grund*, p. 54.

28 Heidegger, *Identität und Differenz*, p. 71.

which the question about God can really be asked.[29] If one does not immediately ask the question about God but first tries to reach clarity concerning the essence of man as related to the unconcealedness of meaning, he does not at all imply that there is no God.[30]

The Term "Cause"

When in a preceding chapter we confronted phenomenology with the inspiration of metaphysics in its first phase, we came to the conclusion that the two do not exclude each other, provided, however, be-ing is not conceived as the "in itself" of representative realism. Because Heidegger had to overcome this form of realism, he devoted his full attention to the phenomenological reduction. It stands to reason, therefore, that Heidegger objects to the fact that traditional metaphysics omits the step by which thinking finds its authentic dimension and, at once, interprets the question regarding the "why" of be-ing as the question about its cause. As we have seen, however, it is not possible to disregard the question of the cause once the phenomenological reduction has been made. It follows, therefore, that metaphysics in the second phase and phenomenology likewise do not exclude each other provided, however, the First Cause is not conceived as the first link of a series, which itself would be represented as a series "in itself."

Many phenomenologists react to the term "cause" in

---

[29] "Wie soll denn der Mensch der gegenwärtigen Weltgeschichte auch nur ernst und streng fragen können, ob der Gott sich nahe oder entziehe, wenn der Mensch es unterlässt, allererst in die Dimensions hineinzudenken, in der jene Frage allein gefragt werden kann." Heidegger, *Ueber den Humanismus,* p. 37.

[30] "Es ist daher nicht nur übereilt, sondern schon im Vorgehen irrig, wenn man behauptet, die Auslegung des Wesens des Menscher aus dem Bezug dieses Wesens zu Wahrheit des Seins sei Atheismus." Heidegger, *ibid,* p. 36.

the same way as to "objective," "rational," "scientific," "reason," "concept," "idea," "demonstration," "universal," "nature," "essence," "absolute," "rational animal," "subject," "object" and many other terms. Some phenomenologists become nervous and excited when these terms are again introduced in a phenomenological philosophy, simply because they have been used before in trends of thinking and systems of philosophy that are rejected by phenomenology. They seem to think that, in order to prevent these rejected conceptions from surreptitiously re-entering the scene, they must reject also all terms that have been used by others and are "infected" by this traditional usage. Anyone who uses such criticized terms is automatically suspected of re-introducing the rejected ideas.

For instance, a certain ethical thinker among our acquaintances objected to the assertion that ethics says: man ought to do the good. Later it appeared that this assertion brought back to his mind the way in which in boarding school he was told to "be good." Heidegger is evidently a metaphysician, but he does not want to be qualified as such because his thinking is metaphysical in a different way from that of traditional metaphysics. Yet "differently metaphysical" is obviously not the same as "non-metaphysical." Likewise, there are phenomenologists who are evidently phenomenological in their thinking but differently from other phenomenologists. Yet some of them do not want to be called "phenomenologists," as if "differently phenomenological" were the same as "non-phenomenological."

The same state of affairs could be illustrated also by means of examples referring to the other above-mentioned rejected terms: "objective," "rational," "scientific," "reason," "idea," "demonstration," "rational animal," "absolute" and many others. Some phenomenologists create confusion and bring discredit to their own way of thinking. They often do not say what they intend to say because they do not want to use certain terms, even if these terms have meanings against which the inspiration of phenomenological thinking cannot have any objections.

One of the most irritating examples of such a confusion-creating attitude occurred in an argument of a phenomenologist with someone who disagreed with him: "Apparently you still admit the principle of contradiction." He may have meant it as a joke, but phenomenologists who indulge in that kind of jokes have no reason to be surprised if others subsequently reproach them for having rejected the principle of contradiction. It is not very difficult to show that there are wrong ways of defending the principle. Phenomenology has contributed its share in pointing out why certain conceptions of that principle are wrong. But if a phenomenologist thinks that someone has such a wrong conception and simply tells him that "apparently he still accepts the principle of contradiction," confusion is bound to arise. What is even worse, others will allege that, being "phenomenologists," they can make the most extravagant statements because they "do not have to worry about the principle of contradiction."

These remarks apply also the use of the terms "cause" and "First Cause." Heidegger rejects them unqualifiedly because, for him, "cause" means a unilateral, deterministic influence "in itself," and "First Cause" means the first within a series "in itself." If, however, these two terms must not be conceived in that way, it does not follow that they cannot have any authentic sense. Metaphysics cannot ask about the cause of be-ing if this cause is conceived as a unilateral, deterministic influence "in itself"; metaphysics cannot affirm a First Cause if this First Cause is conceived as the first within a series "in itself"; nevertheless, it does not follow from this that metaphysics can not at all ask about the cause of meaning as meaning. For Heidegger, however, this conclusion seems to follow. He does not ask about the cause of be-ing, not only not in the way in which this question would be nonsensical but not at all. His failure to ask this question implies that he has not attained the radicalism proper to the inspiration of traditional metaphysics.

Heidegger and Scholastic Metaphysics

For Heidegger it is unqualifiedly certain that scholastic metaphysics is guilty of the "bad" way of regarding God as "First Cause." We doubt, however, that his stand does justice to the inspiration of scholastic metaphysics.[31] Of course, it must be admitted that this inspiration has sometimes lost its authenticity and suffered from degeneration. Nevertheless, it remains true that within the authentic inspiration, of scholastic metaphysics the "Supreme Be-ing" (Summum Ens) was not conceived as the highest within a series of be-ings, and the "First Cause" was not conceived as the first cause within a series of causes. God, as Supreme Be-ing and as First Cause, was "conceived" as absolutely Transcendent and as the absolutely "Other than be-ings." For this reason God was called the Being (Esse).

Within the inspiration of scholastic metaphysics and in the framework of its own terminology, this name is not

---

[31] "When St. Thomas speaks of God as Summum Ens and Summum Bonum, it would be a radical misunderstanding of his intention to think that he wants to speak of 'one of the be-ings, be it the highest,' and 'one of the values, be it the highest.' Summum and Primum are used precisely to express God's Jenseitigkeit, His Transcendence, in diesseitige categories, i.e., in categories of space and time." J. Willemse, "De verborgen God bij Thomas van Aquino," Mens en God, Wijsgerige beschouwingen over het religieuze, Utrecht, 1963, p. 133.

as confusing and as ambiguous as Heidegger would have us believe. In his own terminology be-ing means "brute" reality, the "in itself," and being means truth as unconcealedness, the "in itself for us."[32] The affirmation of being means for Heidegger the making of the phenomenological reduction.[33] However, after making the phenomenological reduction, there is no reason why be-ing may not be understood as "in itself for us" or why God, the Transcendent Origin and Cause of be-ing, should not be called Being. Such a way of speaking would terminologically establish that God is "the Other than be-ing."

Moreover, it must be explicitly added that Heidegger himself does not rigidly adhere to his distinction between be-ing and being.[34] Be-ing is repeatedly spoken of as the term of encounter, unconcealedness, the "in itself for us," the correlate of the intentional movement which *Dasein* itself is; in other words, as precisely that which should be affirmed of being.[35] It would not even be possible to avoid doing this, for it is a contradiction to affirm the "in itself" or to say anything whatsoever about it. The simplest perception and the most primitive affirmation of the "in itself" is *de facto* always concerned not with the "in itself" but with the "in itself for us" or, in Heideg-

---

[32] "Sein - nicht Seiendes - 'gibt es' nur, sofern Wahrheit ist. Und sie ist nur, sofern und solange Dasein ist. Sein und Wahrheit 'sind' gleichursprünglich." Heidegger, *Sein und Zeit,* p. 230.

[33] "Heidegger pense que l'existant brut (*Seiendes*) est entièrement hors des prises des facultés humaines . . . Au contraire, l'être de l'existant (das Sein des Seienden) . . . cela est l'oeuvre du *Dasein* qui, pour cette raison, est dit *source de toute vérité.*" De Waelhens, *La philosophie de Martin Heidegger,* Louvain, 3rd ed., 1948, pp. 248-249.

[34] "La distinction *Seiendes-Sein* - si fondamentale qu'elle soit en principe - n'est pas toujours très assurée." De Waelhens, *ibid,* p. 309.

[35] De Waelhens offers very eloquent examples of this matter. Cf. *op. cit.,* pp. 309-311.

gerian terms, not with be-ing but with being.[36] If, then, one places oneself within the intentionality of phenomenology and makes the phenomenological reduction, the correlate of the metaphysical affirmation may without fear of ambiguity be called be-ing as such.

In the same way there is no reason to fear confusion if, in order to indicate that the Transcendent Origin and Cause of be-ing as be-ing is not itself a be-ing, one calls this Cause Being. Such a terminology does not imply a relapse into the natural attitude, provided any notion of making this Being the highest be-ing within a series of "be-ings in themselves" is resolutely discarded. The "affirmation" of Transcendent Being by scholastic metaphysics is not at all an answer to Heidegger's question about the truth of being. However, it is a reply to a question which Heidegger has not yet raised but which nonetheless may not be neglected. If this point is kept in mind, the "affirmation" of being "conceived" as Transcendent Being contains no ambiguity and is not a source of confusion.

In speaking about the "affirmation" of Transcendent Being, we have constantly placed the term "affirmation" between quotation marks. This was done to indicate that this "affirmation" is a very special, even a unique, kind of affirmation. It should not at all be considered on a par with any other affirmation. The reason is that man can affirm only be-ings and that the Transcendent Being is not a be-ing. Be-ing, however, manifests itself in its being-a-be-ing as a pointer to the "Other than be-ing" because it reveals itself as being only through the "influence" of

---

36 "Je ne puis *parler* de l'existence brute, du *Seiendes,* sans la détruire comme opacité radicale. Dès que j'énonce quoi que ce soit à son sujet, elle se transforme en *Sein.* La distinction *Seiendes-Sein* n'est pas seulement difficile en pratique, elle est insoutenable théoriquement . . . Il est contradictoire de penser au *Seiendes.*" De Waelhens, *ibid.,* p. 309.

the "Other than be-ing." For this reason the affirmation of be-ing is equiprimordially the "affirmation" of the "Other than be-ing." The latter, however, is not a direct affirmation of the Transcendent Being in the way the affirmation of a be-ing is directly concerned with this be-ing because it terminates in this be-ing as a present reality. The direct affirmation of a be-ing is always a kind of "seeing." The "affirmation" of the Transcendent Being, however, is an implication following from man's metaphysical "seeing" but is not itself a way of "seeing." The Transcendent Being reveals itself not as a present reality but only as an implication of such a reality. The "affirmation" of Transcendent Being is directly the affirmation of be-ing as "being from the Other than be-ing." In other words, in the affirmation of be-ing the "Other than be-ing" is merely co-"affirmed."

The "Affirmation" of the Creator

These ideas are definitely to be kept in mind for a correct understanding of what metaphysics in its second phase means when it speak of creation. Be-ing is created, "called forth" from nothing. Of itself be-ing is simply nothing and, if nonetheless it *is*, then it *is* through the "influence" of the "Other than be-ing." If this "influence" were to cease, be-ing would sink again into nothing. These statements are misrepresented when one claims that those who speak of creation start from supposing a situation in which there is absolutely nothing. But, so the objection continues, in such a supposition the being of the one who asks the question or that of his question about be-ing must also be thought away. In that case it is evident that no question can really be asked. Thus it follows that there is no standpoint from which the question about creation can really be asked. To inquire into creation means to "stand" nowhere and to ask no real question.

This is the way in which Karl Marx objected to the idea of creation and which others have voiced after him.[37]

Such a way of representing matters, however, is misleading. Even with respect to creation the philosopher places himself in the "wonder of all wonders": that there is something to see and something to say. This wonder is his own existent subjectivity-as-*Cogito*, and within this subjectivity he must see and say that be-ing *is* but *cannot* be from itself. It *is* therefore from the "Other than be-ing," which means that it is created. In his question about creation the metaphysician does not start by supposing a situation in which there is absolutely nothing, but he begins with the affirmation of, and certitude about, the be-ing which he himself as existent subjectivity is. He does not start from a situation in which it is supposed that nothing is, but from the unmistakable fact that there is something although nothing *could* be if there were nothing but be-ings. The "affirmation" of the Creator is directly nothing but the affirmation of the implications contained in be-ing.

From these considerations it should be evident also in what sense one can say that metaphysics "comes to rest" as in a terminus in the "affirmation" of the Creator. This statement does not mean that the never-finished history of dis-closing that which is said to be is considered to have reached its end. Thinking can never be brought to an end without ceasing to be human thinking. The asser-

---

[37] "Wenn du nach der Schöpfung der Natur und des Menschen fragst, so abstrahierst du also vom Menschen und der Natur. Du setzest sie als *nicht-seiend* und willst doch, dass ich sie als *seiend* dir beweise. Ich sage dir nun: Gib deine Abstraktion auf, so gibst du auch deine Frage auf, oder willst du an deiner Abstraktion festhalten, so sei konsequent, und wenn du den Menschen und die Natur als *nichtseiend* denkend denkst, so denke dich selbst als nicht-seiend, da du doch auch Natur und Mensch bist." K. Marx, *Zur Kritik der Nationalökonomie*, in Marx-Engels, *Kleine ökonomische Schriften*, Berlin, 1955, p. 139.

tion that metaphysics "comes to rest" in that "affirmation" means only that the affirmation of be-ing no longer manifests itself as both necessary and impossible, as it would have to do if the subject-as-*Cogito* would recognize nothing but be-ings. The affirmation of be-ing as be-ing is necessary because be-ing imposes itself unmistakably as be-ing. There is not nothing. On the other hand, the recognition of be-ing is impossible because, as long as one affirms only be-ings, one *de facto* recognizes only "caused" be-ings, and the latter cannot be affirmed as be-ings unless one "affirms" also their "Cause." Accordingly, the "affirmation" of the Creator is a "resting point" only insofar as it makes it possible to maintain the affirmation of be-ing. By the "affirmation" of the Creator the affirmation of metaphysical truth as unconcealedness is safeguarded against contradiction and thereby secured of a future.

Finally we must emphasize that the "affirmation" of the Creator cannot be a ground on which the subject-as-*Cogito* could claim to affirm the universality of be-ings from the standpoint of the Creator. This point is clearly contained in our statement that the "affirmation" of the Creator is directly nothing but the affirmation of be-ing and its implications. When one realizes these implications, one realizes also that the direct affirmation of the universe of be-ings is equiprimordially the indirect "affirmation" of the Creator.

Sometimes also the following difficulty is made. Precisely because phenomenological thinking is phenomenological, it is unable to make this forward step toward recognition of the Creator, under pain of ceasing to be phenomenology. However, such an objection can be raised only by first forcing phenomenology into a strait-jacket precluding that "forward step," and then "concluding" from that restriction that phenomenology as phenomenology cannot make such a move, cannot go beyond certain limits. These limits beyond the reach of phenomenology result from the strait-jacket imposed on phenomenology as allegedly pertaining to its very essence. Daniélou, for example, asserts that phenomenology is essentially defined as the accurate description of concrete human situations.[38] Its limitation, then, is that it is not really a philosophy but only a suitable "nurse maid," guiding man to philosophical thinking. As such, phenomenology may not aspire to substitute itself for philosophy.[39] According to Lotz, the maximum within reach of phenomenology is to affirm historical and finite being. This affirmation demands the recognition of the supra-historical and infinite Being, but this recognition cannot be made by phenomenology itself.[40] Discursive thinking lies beyond the limits of phenomenology as such.[41]

It stands to reason that phenomenological thinking has certain limits. These limits, however, are not the restrictions imposed from without by such aprioristic and "narrow" definitions, but the limits proper to philosophy

---

[38] "Nous devons nous rappeler ici que la phénoménologie de l'existence se définit essentiellement comme étant la description de certaines situations globales dans lesquelles l'homme se trouve ainsi engagé." J. Daniélou, *Le problème de Dieu et l'existentialisme,* p. 29.

[39] "La phénoménologie ne saurait jamais se substituer à la philosophie, á la démarche métaphysique. Elle se cantonne en effet à une description des choses." Daniélou, *ibid.,* p. 34.

[40] "Solange man sich nämlich auf die phänomenologische Analyse beschränkt, kann ein gewisser Umgreis nicht überschritten werden. Die äusserste Grenze des Erreichbaren stellt das geschichtliche und endliche Sein dar. Ob diesem aber ein übergeschichtliches und unendliches Sein, also das Sein Gottes selbst zugrundeliegt, lässt sich bloss phänomenologisch schlechterdings nicht ausmachen." J. Lotz, "Heidegger und das Sein," *Universitas,* vol. VI (1951), p. 843.

[41] Lotz, *ibid.,* p. 844.

itself. For "phenomenology is philosophy itself" (Merleau-Ponty).

3. Metaphysics and the Absolute

The Transcendent Absolute

We have wandered far, so it seems, from our original theme. That theme was the reproach made by some metaphysicians that phenomenology is not and cannot be metaphysics because it rejects the Absolute. As we have already pointed out, a sharp distinction must be made between the Transcendent Absolute, which scholastic metaphysics identifies with God as Origin and Cause of all be-ings, and the absolutized Absolute, of which examples have been given in a preceding chapter.

From our confrontation of phenomenology and metaphysics it has become evident, we hope, that the "primitive" fact or central reference point of phenomenology does not at all make superfluous or impossible the "affirmation" of the Absolute, "conceived" as that which explains everything and itself needs no explanation. The condition, however, for the authenticity of this "affirmation" is that the Absolute be "conceived" as Transcendent. It should not be "understood," to remain close to Heidegger's line of thinking, as a kind of physical cause which is called first within a series "in itself." Only the Transcendent Absolute may be identified with the God of Christian revelation. In the history of human thought attributes that are traditionally "affirmed" of God have been ascribed to the absolutized Absolute; for example, to Fichte's Ego, Haeckel's Nature and Marx's Proletariat. The absolutized Absolute has also been identified with "God." This "God," however, is not the God of Christian revelation, and for this reason the traditional metaphysics of the scholastics has always sharply distinguished its "affirmation" of the Transcendent Absolute from the affirmation of the absolutized Absolute.

All phenomenologists without exception reject the absolutized Absolute. Traditional scholastic metaphysics has no objection against that rejection. Nevertheless, some metaphysicians accuse phenomenology, without any further qualifications, of not being a metaphysics and of being unable to be a metaphysics because phenomenology rejects "the" Absolute. They do not make any distinction between the Transcendent Absolute and the absolutized Absolute when they make this accusation. The reason given for this accusation is that "the" phenomenologists themselves say that the affirmation of the Absolute asphyxiates the "metaphysical" in man. We must now examine what is meant by this statement of "the" phenomenologists.

The "Metaphysical" in Man and the Absolute

When Gusdorf and Merleau-Ponty speak about the "metaphysical" in man, they want to refer to the authenticity of human existence. In their eyes any affirmation of the Absolute implies that man can no longer be affirmed as he should be affirmed. Thus to recognize the Absolute is to disregard man as man.

To recognize what is authentically human implies first of all to affirm man's subjectivity.[42] By means of his subjectivity man rises above the realm of things, so that he is for himself and so that things are for him. Through the emergence of subjectivity the compact density and the impenetrable darkness of things is perforated and marks the beginning of the human history of truth and values. The subject exists as *Cogito* and as *Volo*.

An implication of man's subjectivity is that the reality of man, existing on the proper level of his being-man,

---

[42] Merleau-Ponty, *Sens et Non-sens,* pp. 186-187.

cannot be expressed in terms of models, categories and concepts borrowed from the realm of things. Through his subjectivity man transcends being a thing. The subject cannot be spoken of in terms of necessity. The being of things is a being necessitated, it is nothing but the necessitated result of deterministic processes and forces. The existent subject, on the other hand, transcends the determinism of the cosmos. For this reason, says Merleau-Ponty, any attempt to "explain" the subject is a criminal assault on the subject. Things can be explained, for to explain means to understand in terms of necessitating antecedents.[43] "Explaining" the subject, however, is not possible, for the "explanation" would disregard the subject and deny his authenticity, the "metaphysical" in man. The being of the subject is a not-being-necessitated, a being-contingent.[44]

According to Merleau-Ponty, the subject's contingency is also disregarded if one connects it with, and explains it on the basis of, the Sovereign Necessity of God. The Absolute and the contingency of the subject cannot go together.[45]

Merleau-Ponty evidently places creation on a par with the unilateral and deterministic causality of a physical cause and considers it as if it were the influence of a thing upon another thing. His rejection of the Absolute, of God, does not differ in this respect from the protest of so

[43] "J'ai pris le mot explication dans son sens courant dans la langue philosophique allemande, qui oppose *erklären* et *verstehen.*" Merleau-Ponty, "Deuxième entretien privé," *La connaissance de l'homme au XX*e *siècle, Rencontres internationales de Genève 1952,* p. 246.

[44] "S'il fallait donner à nos précédentes remarques une formule philosophique, nous dirions que notre temps a fait et fait l'expérience de la contingence." Merleau-Ponty, "L'homme et l'adversité," *ibid.,* p. 70.

[45] *Eloge de la philosophie,* pp. 61-63.

many other thinkers who refuse to accept a "God" conceived as the first cause within a series of physical causes. All of them are right, for they object against lowering the Transcendent Absolute. Anyone who conceives God's creation as a kind of explosion of sublimated cosmic energy and "explains" the subject on this basis simply disregards and buries under verbiage the reality which the subject is, the authenticity, the "metaphysical" in man. Let us see, however, what the situation is if the Absolute is "conceived" as Transcendent.

Two Senses of Contingency

For Merleau-Ponty it is contingency that characterizes the mode of being of the subject. The being of the subject is a being-contingent because and to the extent that the subject cannot be the result of deterministic processes and forces. For otherwise the subject would be a thing just as all results of processes and forces. But in that case there would be no meaning, for a thing is not a meaning for another thing. Meaning, however, *is* because the contingent subject is. Being-contingent, therefore, means for Merleau-Ponty not-being-necessitated in the way the being of things must be called a being-necessitated. To be contingent is to be free. The contingency of the subject has an anthropological sense for Merleau-Ponty.

In traditional metaphysics, however, the term "contingency" is used in a different and more profound sense. The metaphysician says that be-ing as be-ing is contingent to convey that any be-ing, precisely as a be-ing, does not have a sufficient ground for its being in itself. From an anthropological standpoint the being of the subject must be called a being-contingent or being-free, and the being of a thing a being-necessitated. From a metaphysical standpoint, however, both the subject and the thing, considered as be-ings, as not-nothing, are called "contingent" because as mere be-ings they do not have the ground of their being in themselves. The same term, therefore, assumes different senses in different perspectives. For Merleau-Ponty the subject's contingency means not to be necessitated by processes and forces, i.e., to be free. For traditional metaphysics a be-ing's contingency means that it does not have within itself the explanatory ground of being, which applies to both the subject and the thing insofar as both are be-ings, not-nothing.

This difference explains also why the metaphysicians continue their inquiry and search for an all-encompassing and all-explanatory principle while Merleau-Ponty does not at all feel called to make such a search. The metaphysicians have to continue their inquiry because their metaphysical affirmation of be-ing as be-ing suddenly reveals itself as an impossibility as long as they affirm nothing else but be-ing. For the latter reveals itself as without a ground in itself and therefore as entirely unable to be if there is nothing but be-ings. In this perspective of thinking nothing suddenly reveals itself as much more simple than be-ing. However, one cannot say that there is nothing, for be-ings are and unmistakably so. In this way the metaphysicians arrive at a point where they have to say either that nothing is or that the affirmation of be-ings contains a new dimension since they *cannot* be from themselves. Nevertheless, there are be-ings; therefore, the "Other than be-ing," the Transcendent Being "is."

With respect to both Heidegger and Merleau-Ponty the same remark must be made, viz., they do not go beyond establishing the proper "climate" for authentic thinking. Authentic thinking demands that the subject's intentionality be recognized and the phenomenological reduction made. But this same thinking may not disregard the question of the "why" of be-ing, understood as the question about the Cause, for be-ing manifests itself as not having a ground for its being in itself and as nonetheless being. The answer to this question about the ground of be-ings is found in the "affirmation" of the Transcendent Being as an implication of the affirmation of be-ings; in other words, as an implication of the "metaphysical" in man.[46] The "metaphysical" in man is choked to death by the Absolute only if the Absolute is not "conceived" as Transcendent.

The Absolute as "Truth Itself" and "Goodness Itself"

The "metaphysical" in man, the authenticity of human existence, can be disregarded in many ways and not only by conceiving creation as a kind of explosion of sublimated cosmic energy and regarding the Transcendent Being as a first physical cause within a chain of physical causes.

Above we have seen that the being of the subject is a being-contingent in the anthropological sense of the term.[47] Because the subject is contingent, human history is not a deterministic process. The contingent subject is the source from which the history of truth and of values flows. Truth emerges in the subject's act of dis-closing and values are founded by the subject as replies to demands contained in existence. Since, however, history is not a process, the dis-closure of truth and the founding of values lack the necessity and guarantee of a natural process. A natural process always "turns out well," that is, it al-

---

[46] In another sense than the one intended by Heidegger, we must say: "Die Metaphysik ist das Grundgeschehen im Dasein. Sie ist das Dasein selbst." Heidegger, *Was ist Metaphysik?*, p. 41.

[47] "Tout est contingence dans l'homme . . . L'homme est une idée historique et non pas une espèce naturelle." *Phénoménologie de la perception,* p. 199..

ways turns out as it should because it is "guaranteed" by the necessity which governs natural forces. Hence, strictly speaking, we expressed ourselves incorrectly when we said that history "lacks" the necessity of a natural process.[48] History is history precisely because it is not a process, because the necessity governing the cosmos is "perforated" by the subject.[49] Man is not a "force" but a "weakness."[50]

This "weakness" of the subject is his contingency. It implies that history can "turn out badly." The acceptance of this possibility is included in the recognition of what man *is*, viz., a human be-ing. For this reason the history of man's dis-closure of truth and his founding of values is precarious and full of risks. "Progress" does not come about of necessity and is not guaranteed. It is not excluded that man may fail midway, like an unfinished grammatical sentence.[51] This idea may cause vertigo when one reflects upon its awesome possibility. It has led some to ask Merleau-Ponty whether man can live in such a dizzy atmosphere. His answer is eloquent: "Philosophy is not a hospital."[52] Someone who suffers from dizziness can take medicine to cure his vertigo. He can do the same when being-man makes him dizzy. Yet if he does so, he slinks away from himself, he disregards himself, commits treason against his authenticity and obscures the "metaphysical" of his being-man.

---

[48] "La contingence de l'événement humain n'est plus maintenant comme un défaut dans la logique de l'histoire, elle en devient la condition." Merleau-Ponty, *Eloge de la philosophie,* p. 71.

[49] "L'histoire n'a pas de sens si son sens est compris comme celui d'une rivière qui coule sous l'action de causes toutes-puissantes vers un océan où elle disparait." *Ibid.,* p. 71.

[50] *Ibid.,* p. 61.

[51] Merleau-Ponty, "L'homme et l'adversité," *La connaissance de l'homme au XXe siècle,* p. 71.

[52] Merleau-Ponty, "Deuxième entretien privé," *ibid.,* p. 247.

According to Merleau-Ponty, both Marxism and Christianity are guilty in this matter. For the Marxist history is a process, and he thinks that in his actions he takes part in a process that of necessity "turns out well." He disregards man's contingency, the "metaphysical" in man's contingency, the "metaphysical" in man. The Christian also is guilty of the same mistake. Because the Christian adheres to the Absolute as "Truth itself" and "Goodness itself," he considers himself entitled to evaluate the contingent search for truth and the contingent founding of values from without, from a standpoint that is not the standpoint of a contingent subject. Thus man's search is no longer important and the *real* life of truth and of values is buried under verbiage. The Christian thinks that he can speak and act with "divine right." He lapses of necessity into fixism, dogmatism and intolerance. He also disregards the "metaphysical" in man.

In Chapter Two we have described in detail the view of Merleau-Ponty, which is shared by Gusdorf. Both reject the affirmation of the Absolute in order to safeguard the "metaphysical" in man.

One who does not want to be guided by mere words should realize that great prudence is needed with respect to the reproach that phenomenology cannot be a metaphysics because it rejects the Absolute. True, the most prominent phenomenologists themselves say so. However, what exactly do they say? They claim that the affirmation of the Absolute, of God, does not offer man any guarantee in his contingent search for truth and his contingent founding of values. They add that if, in spite of this, one ascribes a "divine right" to his actions, he disregards the authenticity of man's being and chokes it to death. Undoubtedly, all this is true. Nevertheless, we must add that anyone who disregards the human character of man in such a way demonstrates that he has no notion of

God's Transcendence. When man tries to be God's master and to put Him on his side as a guarantee of his deeds, he demolishes God's Transcendence. He disregards both God and man. The fact that some phenomenologists reject "the" Absolute is a warning for phenomenology to be more prudent than others have been in the past when it wants to develop into a metaphysics and "affirm" the Absolute.

CHAPTER FIVE

PERSPECTIVES

At the beginning of this book we mentioned that we are
interested in the inspiration of traditional metaphysics
because of the possibilities contained in its way of thinking. One of these possibilities is the so-called "proof" for
the existence of God.

We do not wish to claim, however, that the road to God
opened by traditional metaphysics is the only possible
approach. Many thinkers prefer to rely upon a description of the phenomenon of religiousness, in which use is
made of the age-old wisdom contained in myths or in
which the emphasis is placed upon the explicitation of
"pointers" to God in the use of symbols. While we do not
at all want to deny the value of such approaches, we
asked ourselves whether it is possible to make use of
them without, at least implicitly, relying upon an authentic metaphysics.

The reason for this question is as follows: in the description of the phenomenon of religiousness the distinction between authentic religiousness and pseudo-religiousness, between God and pseudo-gods, will inevitably impose itself. Yet we do not see where one could find a
rational basis for this distinction if it is not sought in an
authentic metaphysics. A description of the phenomenon
of "the" religiousness of man in which no role is assigned

to the distinction between authentic religiousness and pseudo-religiousness offers us no ground for confidence with respect to the attempt to find a road to the authentic God. The authentic or true God is the Transcendent God. Descriptions of things that are strictly pseudo-religious do not constitute roads of approach to the Transcendent God.

1. *Being as "Initiative"*

The preceding chapters did not intend to insinuate that the road to God sought by Heidegger does not lead anywhere. They indicated what traditional metaphysics must learn from Heidegger if, faithful to its own inspiration, it wants to be what it is able to be—namely, a rational justification of the "affirmation" of God. Solely for this reason we made use of Heidegger's idea concerning the distinction between being and be-ing, understood as meaning and "brute" reality. Let us repeat, therefore, once more that his theory of being contains more than the ideas utilized in the preceding chapters. We have hardly spoken, for example, about the return of the distinction between being and be-ing after Heidegger's phenomenological reduction. We have not even mentioned what he could possibly mean concerning the "favor of being" (*Gunst des Seins*) and the inner connection between thinking and thanking.[1]

Likewise we have not spoken of the " 'mission' of being" (*Geschick des Seins*),[2] on which, according to Hei-

---

[1] Heidegger, *Was ist Metaphysik?*, p. 49.

[2] Heidegger, *Identität und Differenz,* p. 72. The term *"Geschick"* is etymologically connected with *geschehen* (to happen), *Geschichte* (history), *schicken* (to send), and *Schickzal* (fortune). All these words are somehow connoted in Heidegger's use of the term *"Geschick."* It refers to an event by which being "sends" (*schickt*) itself to man and as such becomes "com-mitted" to him.

degger, it will depend whether or not mankind will succeed in finding the road back from metaphysics to the essence of metaphysics and from "representative" thinking to authentic thinking.[3] The success will not be decided by man himself but depends upon the history of being itself. Heidegger even adds that forgetfulness of being[4] and overcoming this forgetfulness is the "mission" of being itself.[5] One gets the impression, and not incorrectly, that, with respect to both the forgetfulness of being and overcoming this forgetfulness, the "initiative" lies on the side of being[6] rather than of man,[7] at least in the later

---

The various "missions" of being and the resulting "com-mitments" to man together constitute history. (Tr.)

[3] "Niemand kann wissen, ob und wann und wie dieser Schritt des Denkens zu einem eigentlichen . . . Weg und Gang und Wegebau sich entfaltet. Es könnte sein, dass die Herrschaft der Metaphysik sich eher verfestigt und zwar in der Gestalt der modernen Technik und deren unabsehbaren rasenden Entwicklungen. Es könnte auch sein, dass alles, was sich auf dem des Schrittes zurück ergibt, von der fortbestehenden Metaphysik auf ihre Weise als Ergebnis eines vorstellenden Denkens nur genützt und verarbeitet wird." Heidegger, *ibid.,* p. 71.

[4] "Die Vergessenheit des Seins gehört in das durch sie selbst verhüllte Wesen des Seins. Sie gehört so wesentlich in das Geschick des Seins, dass . . ." Heidegger, *Holzwege,* p. 336.

[5] "Geschick aber ist wesenhaft Geschick des Seins, so zwar, dass das Sein selber sich schickt und je als ein Geschick west und demgemäss sich geschicklich wandelt." Heidegger, *Die Technik und die Kehre,* Pfullingen, 1962, p. 38.

[6] "Uberdies aber ist der Entwurf wesenhaft ein geworfener. Das Werfende im Entwerfen ist nicht der Mensch, sondern das Sein selbst, das den Menschen in die Ek-sistenz des Da-seins als Sein Wesen schickt. Dieses Geschick ereignet sich als die Lichtung des Seins, als welche es ist. Sie gewährt die Nähe zum Sein. In dieser Nähe, in der Lichtung des 'Da' wohnt der Mensch als der Eksistierende, ohne dass er es heute schon vermag, dieses Wohnen eigens zu erfahren und zu übernehmen." Heidegger, *Ueber den Humanismus,* p. 25.

[7] "Wenn das Wesen der Technik, das Gestell als die Gefahr im Sein, das Sein selbst ist, dann lässt sich die Technik niemals durch

Heidegger. There is a unity of reciprocal implication of *Dasein* and being. Within this unity the coming of being occurs and man himself is the "dwelling" in being as the "nearby."

Man, however, has not yet any authentic awareness of what the "dwelling" in being is which he himself is; hence being itself remains "something that is not yet spoken."[8] Future thinking will have to teach us to experience what being is.[9] For the present it will be very difficult to express what being is because man is still very badly equipped for this task. For all the terms which traditional metaphysics used in its efforts to say what being is are terms of a metaphysics which lived in forgetfulness of being.[10] This is the reason, Heidegger says, why he was unable to finish his *Being and Time*.[11] This reason does not make sense to anyone who regards language merely as the expression of a thought that is "finished" in man's interiority without the aid of language.[12] Language, however, actually is the embodiment of thinking, in which man's thinking becomes itself. A new mode of thinking demands of necessity a new mode of speaking. For this reason, says Heidegger, to continue to use the antiquated mode of speaking makes the new mode of thinking impossible.[13]

---

ein bloss auf sich gestelltes menschliches Tun meistern, weder positiv noch negativ. Die Technik, deren Wesen das Sein selbst ist, lässt sich durch den Mensch niemals überwinden. Das hiesse doch: der Mensch sei der Herr des Seins." Heidegger, *Die Technik und die Kehre,* p. 38.

[8] Heidegger, *Was ist Metaphysik ?,* p. 9.

[9] Heidegger, *Ueber den Humanismus,* p. 19.

[10] Heidegger, *Identität und Differenz,* p. 72

[11] Heidegger, *Ueber den Humanismus,* p. 17.

[12] Heidegger, *Was ist das - die Philosophie ?,* p. 44.

[13] "Allein die Frage nach dem Wesen des Seins stirbt ab, wenn sie die Sprache der Metaphysik nicht aufgibt, weil das metaphy-

The forgetfulness of being must be overcome by reflecting upon being as truth, conceived as unconcealedness.[14] The self-manifestation of being and its coming close to man, however, do not occur through an "initiative" of man but of being itself. Man does not decide whether being will manifest itself as truth and whether being, by manifesting itself, will lead him to the truth in his own essence.[15] "The coming of be-ing depends upon the 'mission' of being."[16]

By using such expressions, Heidegger certainly does not intend to deny the relationship of being to man's essence which he has so often affirmed in other texts.[17] Authentic thinking brings the relationship of being to man's essence to completion. It does not "make" or "produce" this relationship, but finds itself having it.[18] For this reason it remains true that being "belongs" to man, for only with man can being "be present" (an-wesen).[19]

Accordingly, the fact that Heidegger sometimes

sische Vorstellen es verwehrt, die Frage nach dem Wesen des Seins zu denken." Heidegger, *Zur Seinsfrage*, p. 26.

14 '*Alētheia* könnte das Wort sein, das einen noch nicht erfahrenen Wink in das ungedachte Wesen des esse gibt." Heidegger, *Was ist Metaphysik ?*, p. 11.

15 "Der Mensch ist vielmehr vom Sein selbst in die Wahrheit des Seins 'geworfen', dass er, dergestalt ek-sistierend, die Wahrheit des Seins hüte, damit im Lichte des Seins das Seiende als das Seiende, das es ist, erscheine. Ob und wie es erscheint, ob und wie der Gott und die Götter, die Geschichte und die Natur in die Lichtung des Seins hereinkommen, an- und abwesen, entscheidet nicht der Mensch." Heidegger, *Ueber den Humanismus*, p. 19.

16 Heidegger, *ibid.*, p. 19.

17 "Aber - sobald ich denkend sage 'Menschenwesen', habe ich darin schon den Bezug zum Sein gesagt. Insgleichen, sobald ich denkend sage: Sein des Seienden, ist darin schon den Bezug zum Menschenwesen genannt." Heidegger, *Was heisst Denken ?*, p. 74.

18 Heidegger, *Ueber den Humanismus*, p. 5.

19 Heidegger, *Identität und Differenz*, p. 24.

ascribes more "initiative" to being than to man does not
mean that he conceives the history of being as a kind of
process which simply "runs its course."[20] Neither is it
a kind of fate that befalls man without man.[21] Heidegger
does not hypostatize being, for even in his later works
the essence of man "belongs" to the essence of being.[22]
Man must "expect" and "wait for" the coming of being.
This is all he can do. Perhaps, says Heidegger, we are
already in the shadow which "the reversal" casts ahead
of itself.[23] No one, however, knows when this "reversal"
will occur. But it is not necessary to know this. Such
knowledge would even be extremely dangerous for man.
For it belongs to his essence to be "waiting," to "expect"
the essence of being while as its "shepherd" he guards
it.[24] He must not try to overpower it with his calcula-

---

[20] "Das Geschick des Seins ist nämlich nicht nur kein an sich
ablaufender Prozess, es ist auch nichts, was uns gegenüber liegt."
Heidegger, *Der Satz vom Grund*, p. 158.

[21] "Aber das Fatum ist als der Spruch des Seins im Sinne des
sich entziehenden Geschickes nichts fatalistisches . . . Weshalb
nicht ? Weil Sein, indem es sich zuschickt, das Freie des Zeit-
Spiel-Raumes erbringt und in einem damit den Menschen erst ins
Freie seiner jeweils schicklichen Wesensmöglichkeiten befreit."
Heidegger, *ibid.*, p. 158.

[22] "Weil jedoch das Sein sich als Wesen der Technik in das
Gestell geschickt hat, zum Wesen des Seins aber das Menschenwesen gehört, insofern das Wesen des Seins das Menschenwesen
braucht, um als Sein nach dem eigenen Wesen inmitten des Seienden *gewahrt* zu bleiben und so *als* das Sein zu wesen, deshalb kann
das Wesen der Technik nicht ohne die Mithilfe des Menschenwe-
sens in den Wandel seines Geschickes geleitet werden." Heidegger,
Die Technik und die Kehre, p. 38.

[23] Heidegger, *ibid.*, pp. 40-41.

[24] "Wann und wie sie sich geschicklich ereignet, weiss niemand.
Es ist auch nicht nötig, solches zu wissen. Ein Wissen dieser Art
wäre sogar das Verderblichste für den Menschen, weil sein Wesen
ist, der Wartende zu sein, der des Wesens des Seins wartet, indem
er es denkend hütet. Nur wenn der Mensch als der Hirt des Seins
der Wahrheit des Seins wartet, kann er eine Ankunft des Seins-

tions.[25] Accordingly, the "mission" of being is also equiprimordially the "mission" of thinking.[26]

2. *The Sense of the Sacred in Heidegger*

According to Heidegger, the question whether man will find again a road to God will not depend upon man himself but upon the "mission" of being.[27] Traditional metaphysics, living in forgetfulness of being, has not only made the interpretation of being very difficult but has also defended atheism, in spite of the fact that it constantly spoke about "God." Its speaking about God was merely a speaking about a pseudo-god. If, then, it is already so difficult to transcend metaphysics by taking the "step back" to the essence of metaphysics, there is every reason, Heidegger says, to remain provisionally silent about God. Because traditional thinking about God is metaphysics and metaphysics must be transcended, man's thinking is not yet able to indicate what the term "God" means.[28]

---

geschickes erwarten, ohne in das blosse Wisenwollen zu verfallen." Heidegger, *ibid.*, p. 41.

[25] Heidegger *ibid.*, pp. 45-46.

[26] Heidegger, *Ueber den Humanismus,* p. 46.

[27] "Ob der Gott lebt oder tot bleibt, entscheidet sich nicht durch die Religiosität der Menschen und noch weniger durch theologische Aspirationen der Philosophie und der Naturwissenschaft. Ob Gott Gott ist, ereignet sich aus der Konstellation des Seins und innerhalb ihrer. Solange wir nicht denkend erfahren, was ist, können wir nie dem gehören, was sein wird." Heidegger, *Die Technik und die Kehre,* p. 46.

[28] "Wer die Theologie, sowohl diejenige des christlichen Glaubens als auch diejenige der Philosophie, aus gewachsener Herkunft erfahren hat, zieht es heute vor, im Bereich des Denkens von Gott zu schweigen. Denn der onto-theologische Charakter der Metaphysik ist für das Denken fragwürdig geworden, nicht auf Grund irgendeines Atheismus, sondern aus der Erfahrung eines Denkens, dem sich in der Onto-Theologie die noch *ungedachte* Ein-

Accordingly, Heidegger does not claim that the road to God is inaccessible for the philosopher. The road is impossible for traditional metaphysics and extremely difficult even for authentic thinking. It will be rediscovered when man's thinking rediscovers its proper dimension, when it develops as a thinking of the truth of being. From the truth of being man can go on to thinking of the essence of the sacred, and only from the essence of the sacred can he go on to thinking of the essence of the Divinity, and only in the light of the essence of the Divinity can he think and say what the term "God" means.[29]

Reflection, therefore, upon the sacred is for Heidegger the road to authentic thinking about God. Perhaps, he adds, the only misfortune of our era lies in the fact that the dimension of the sacred has become closed to us.[30] It has made God and the gods escape from us. Heidegger regards Hölderlin as the poet *par excellence* of God's absence.[31] The poets are called to give voice again to the sacred,[32] in order to prepare the coming of God.

---

heit des Wesens der Metaphysik gezeigt hat." Heidegger, *Identität und Differenz,* p. 51.

[29] "Erst aus der Wahrheit des Seins lässt sich das Wesen des Heiligen denken. Erst aus dem Wesen des Heiligen ist das Wesen von Gottheit zu denken. Erst im Lichte des Wesens von Gottheit kann gedacht und gesagt werden, was das Wort 'Gott' nennen soll." Heidegger, *Ueber den Humanismus,* pp. 36-37.

[30] Heidegger, *ibid.,* p 37.

[31] "Indem Hölderlin das Wesen der Dichtung neu stiftet, bestimmt er erst eine neue Zeit. Es ist die Zeit der entflohenen Götter und des kommenden Gottes. Das ist die dürftige Zeit, weil sie in einem gedoppelten Mangel und Nicht steht: im Nichtmehr der entflohenen Götter und im Nochnicht des Kommenden." Heidegger, *Erläuterungen zu Hölderlins Dichtung,* p. 44.

[32] "Der Denker sagt das Sein. Der Dichter denkt das Heilige." Heidegger, *Was ist Metaphysik ?,* p. 51.

Their poetic voice lets the Lofty One Himself appear.[33] The appearing of God consists in a dis-closing that lets man see what is concealed. However, it does not let us see the concealed by tearing it loose from its concealment but by guarding it in its self-concealment.[34] The unknown God appears as the Unknown.[35]

We must repeat here what we have said above: the fact that we make no effort to interpret here Heidegger's remarkable texts about the "mission" of being and its bearing upon the approach to God should not be taken to insinuate that no positive results can be expected of the way to God which Heidegger himself wants to take. Our sole intention is to show that under certain conditions the "primitive fact" of phenomenology is not a conflict with the inspiration of traditional metaphysics.

Meanwhile critique of Heidegger has not been lacking. It has come from many sides, but finds its most profound expression in E. Levinas. We will consider his critique in the following section.

3. *The Metaphysics of Levinas*

Subjectivity and the Western Tradition of Thinking

With increasing firmness Heidegger has drawn main lines through the history of philosophy in order to characterize entire eras of philosophical thinking and even to understand the tradition of metaphysics in its inmost essence. Levinas tries to arrive at a similar understanding of Heidegger's thinking. What, ultimately, is the charac-

---

33 "Dichtend nennen bedeutet: im Wort den Hohen selbst erscheinen lassen." Heidegger, *Erläuterungen zu Hölderlins Dichtung,* p. 26.

34 Heidegger, *Vorträge und Aufsätze,* p. 197.

35 "So erscheint der unbekannte Gott als der Unbekannte durch die Offenbarkeit des Himmels." Heidegger, *ibid.,* p. 197.

ter of Heidegger's way of thinking? Within the inspiration of Heidegger's thinking what, ultimately, is contained in the totality of everything that, no matter how, is said to *be?* What, in the last resort, is the scope of the term "being" as it is used by Heidegger?

According to Levinas, Heidegger's thinking does not differ from the constant tradition of Western thought. The entire tradition of the West has always conceived the subject solely as called to overpower and possess the totality of being through his thinking.[36] No wonder, then, that war occurs so frequently in the West.[37]

This Western inspiration of thinking assumes a clearcut and specific form in idealism, which sacrifices the autonomy of being that meaning has to the absolutized Subject. Heidegger has always resisted idealism, but this does not mean that he has managed to escape from the general tendency of Western thinking to overpower and possess being.

The inspiration of Western thinking allows only that aspect of being to present itself which lets itself be overpowered and possessed without being thereby deprived of its own character. If there were realities which by their very nature do not let themselves be mastered and possessed, they would be eliminated from the totality of being by the inspiration of a philosophy that wants to master and possess. In that case such a philosophy would be defective.

---

[36] "La philosophie occidentale a été le plus souvent une ontologie: une réduction de l'Autre au Même, par l'entremise d'un terme moyen et neutre qui assure l'intelligence de l'être." E. Levinas, *Totalité et Infini, Essai sur l'extériorité,* La Haye, 1961, p. 13.

[37] "La face de l'être qui se montre dans la guerre, se fixe dans le concept de totalité qui domine la philosophie occidentale." Levinas, *ibid.,* Préface, p. X.

According to Levinas, this defect exists in Heidegger's philosophy. Heidegger shows himself insensitive to an event that is entirely new with respect to the inspiration of Western thinking and which Levinas described as the "epiphany of the visage" (*l'épiphanie du visage*).[38] This term refers to the appearing of our fellow-man's countenance, the emergence of the other's subjectivity, with respect to which all overpowering and possessing operates destructively.[39] Through the emergence of the other as subject and in the light of the value of the other's subjectivity, any form of thinking encompassed by the tendency to overpower and possess its object reveals itself as a criminal assault upon mankind. The regard of the stranger, the widow or the orphan places man's thinking in an entirely new dimension. According to Levinas, Heidegger has failed to see this. The way in which he speaks the term "is" is such that it eliminates the being of the stranger, the widow and the orphan. The "call" (*Zuspruch*) of being is for him identical with what is "present" (*an-west*) to him, the hermit of the Black Forest, viz., the mildness of ears of wheat and the harshness of a rocky cliff (Dondeyne). Man as *Dasein* takes part in bringing about the truth of being, but, says Levinas, Heidegger attaches no ethical importance to this. The "epiphany of the visage" and the demands implied by it play no role in Heidegger's philosophy.[40]

---

[38] Levinas, *ibid., passim.*

[39] "Ce regard qui supplie et exige . . . ce regard est précisément l'épiphanie du visage comme visage. La nudité du visage est dénûment. Reconnaître autrui, c'est reconnaître une faim. Reconnaître Autrui - c'est donner. Mais c'est donner au maître, au seigneur, à celui que l'on aborde comme 'vous' dans une dimension de hauteur." Levinas, *ibid.*, p. 48.

[40] "Regard de l'étranger, de la veuve et de l'orphelin et que je ne peux reconnaître qu'en donnant ou qu'en refusant, libre de donner ou de refuser, mais passant nécessairement par l'entremise des choses. Les choses ne sont pas, comme chez Heidegger, le fon-

Levinas presents his own philosophy as a plea for subjectivity, but not for the kind that is encompassed by an egoistic protest against reality or by dread of death.[41] The authentic subject is the subject who receives the other subject as another subject. For this reason authentic metaphysical thinking is primarily an ethical thinking.[42]

The dimension of the divine opens itself to Levinas in the recognition of the other's subjectivity.[43] In and through goodness and justice toward men God reveals Himself as Presence.[44] Divorced from the relationship to other human beings there can be no "knowledge" of God.[45] The other subject is the "place" of metaphysical knowledge, for the "epiphany of his visage" is "the manifestation of the heights where God reveals Himself."[46]

Other Modes of Metaphysical Thinking and the Principle of Causality

This summary and rather sketchy characterization of Levinas' thinking is offered here merely to show that contemporary metaphysical reflection continues to retain the inspiration of traditional thought. Metaphysics is concerned with making an attempt to present an "account"

---

dement du lieu, la quinte-essence de toutes les relations qui constituent notre présence sur terre (et 'sous le ciel, en compagnie des hommes et dans l'attente des dieux'). C'est la rapport du Même avec l'Autre, c'est mon accueil de l'Autre, qui est le fait ultime et où surviennent les choses non pas comme ce qu'on édifie, mais comme ce qu'on donne." Levinas, *ibid.,* p. 49.

[41] Levinas, *ibid.,* Préface, XIV.

[42] Levinas, *ibid.,* p. 13.

[43] "La dimension du divin s'ouvre à partir du visage humain." Levinas, *ibid.,* p. 50.

[44] Levinas, *ibid.,* p. 50.

[45] "Il ne peut y avoir, séparée de la relation avec les hommes, aucune 'connaissance' de Dieu." Levinas, *ibid.,* p. 51.

[46] Levinas, *ibid.,* p. 51.

of "everything" and has two phases.[47] In its second phase man's thinking tries to reach the Absolute, which, as Absolute, "explains" everything and itself does not need to be explained. Scholastic metaphysics has given a certain form to this thinking and in this form the principle of "causality" plays a crucial role. In the preceding pages we have defended the validity of this scholastic undertaking, without, however, rejecting other modes of metaphysical thinking. Levinas' philosophy, which shows a certain analogy with the metaphysics of Blondel and Marcel, is such another mode.

The question, however, is whether these other modes of thinking metaphysically, which seemingly do not make use of the principle of "causality," can really show the "necessity" of what they say about the Absolute without the principle of "causality." The Absolute is called "God," who is said to be Transcendent or Infinite. But is it possible to justify precisely this Transcendence without recourse to the principle of "causality"?

To remain far from anything recalling the bad "proofs" and bad conceptions of "causality" proposed in the past, some metaphysicians try to find other ways to the "affirmation" of God than those followed by the metaphysicians of the past. They are, and rightly so, very critical of this past, but often go so far as to reject any idea of "proof" or of "causality." Yet it is dismaying to see how glibly some of them proceed from there. From the absolute dimension of the demands of ethics, from the absolute dimension present in the life of truth, and from the "fullness" implied in loving togetherness they "leap," effortlessly it seems, to God's absolute Transcendence.

We do not intend here to follow these other ways in detail, but merely want to voice a certain skepticism re-

---

[47] A. Dondeyne, "Inleiding tot het denken van E. Levinas," *Tijdschrift voor Philosophie,* vol. XXV (1963), pp. 555-584.

garding the possibility of making a rational justification for the "leap" that is always made. By "rational" justification we do not mean, of course, what rationalism and scientism mean when they speak of "reason." Yet even if one does not take "reason" in a rationalistic or scientistic sense, one cannot escape from speaking of reason in this context. At least not if one does not want the "leap" to be conceived as something that is entirely left to the purely arbitrary choice of the subject. Differently expressed, one who makes the "leap" cannot at the same time claim that the others who do not "leap" are also right. He who makes the "leap" will have to adduce some "reason" why it is "necessary" to "leap." Hence the explicitation of the road leading to the "affirmation" of God's absolute Transcendence will have to include a certain "necessity of thinking." For otherwise those who risk the "leap" can no longer justify why they do not refuse to "leap." They would have no reasons to assume that others who refuse to "leap" would not be just as "right" as they themselves are.

We ask ourselves whether an explicitation of the "necessity of thinking" of which there is question here can be made entirely without recourse to the principle of "causality." This term is then, of course, not used in the sense in which it occurs in the sciences, nor is the "proof" explicitating the "necessity of thinking" similar to a scientific proof. All we want to say is that one who does not want to hear of "proof" or "causality" in *any* sense runs the risk of eliminating *every* "necessity of thinking."

We want to express the same skepticism with respect to the road Heidegger thinks he should follow to approach God. Authentic thinking of being and of the sacred are for him the approach to the "affirmation" of God. He wants to have nothing to do with the principle of "causality." In the light of the accepted scientistic interpretation of this principle, Heidegger's aversion can be understood. However, he rejects the principle of "causality" in any of its interpretations. Is this perhaps the reason why he has not yet managed to "affirm" God as a philosopher?

4. *Philosophy, Theology, and Heidegger*

Heidegger's commentators used to be uncertain whether or not, to judge by his philosophy, he should be called an atheist. Sartre called him a representative of atheistic existentialism, but neglected to indicate how he managed to solve the question which caused Heidegger's commentators so much trouble.[48] However, from the works published by Heidegger after *Being and Time* it has become evident that Sartre was wrong.

Heidegger has had to defend himself against gross misunderstandings in this matter. The fact that he called man's essence "existence" led some of his critics to think that he wanted to substitute man for God. This misconception arose because traditional metaphysics conceived God's essence as *existentia* while Heidegger said that man's essence was existence.[49] These critics did not realize or did not want to see that for Heidegger the term "existence" indicated man's mode of being precisely as distinct from those of things and of God. He wanted to emphasize that man should *not* be deified by philosophy since man's being is a being in the world and that of God most decidedly is not a being in the world. "God is but does not exist."[50] Heidegger is not an atheist.

---

[48] J. P. Sartre, *L'existentialisme est un humanisme,* Paris, 1947, p. 17.

[49] "Die letzte Verirrung wäre jedoch, wollte man den Satz über das eksistente Wesen des Menschen so erklären, als sei er die säkularisierte Uebertragung eines von der christlichen Theologie über Gott ausgesagten Gedankens (Deus est suum esse) auf den Menschen." Heidegger, *Ueber den Humanismus,* pp. 16-17.

[50] Heidegger, *Was ist Metaphysik ?,* p. 15.

Rejection of Pseudo-gods

If there were any doubt left about Heidegger's theism, the way in which he rejects pseudo-gods and defends the authentic "affirmation" of the true God should remove any lingering suspicion. First of all, Heidegger explicitly rejects Hegel's "God." The dialectic process of the recovery of meaning, through which in Hegel's philosophy "God" becomes himself, is for Heidegger identical with the process through which the true God dies. "God" is dead, but, Heidegger adds, this does not mean that there is no God.[51]

Secondly, Heidegger agrees with Nietzsche's rejection of "God," but here also the reason is that Nietzsche rejects a pseudo-god. According to Heidegger, Nietzsche's "God" is somewhat like the suprasensible world in the Platonic sense, a world which for centuries has been accepted as the true, proper and rational world in opposition to the changeable, deceptive and unreal world here below.[52] The latter was called a "valley of tears" in contrast with the lofty heights of happiness in the other world. But, says Nietzsche, this happy world has become powerless, it is unable to inspire man any longer and resuscitate him to new life. "God is dead."[53] Against this "dead God" Nietzsche places the "Superman" and his "will to power."

For Heidegger, however, the death of "God" does not mean that man substitutes himself for God. That would

[51] "Die Wissenschaft der Phänomenologie des Geistes ist die Theologie des Absoluten hinsichtlich seiner Parusie im dialektischspekulativen Karfreitag. Hier stirbt das Absolute. Gott ist tot. Das sagt alles andere, nur nicht: es gibt keinen Gott." Heidegger, *Holzwege*, p. 186.

[52] Heidegger, *ibid.*, pp. 199-200.

[53] "Das Wort 'Gott ist tot' bedeutet: die übersinnliche Welt ist ohne wirkende Kraft. Sie spendet kein Leben. Die Metaphysik . . . ist zu Ende." Heidegger, *ibid.*, p. 200.

be mere foolishness.[54] This death, he says, means that the metaphysics which since Plato has lived in forgetfulness of being is in the throes of death. The place which "God" occupied in this metaphysics can remain vacant.[55] Nietzsche delivered the death blow to metaphysics, but his own thinking was not a transcending of metaphysics. According to Heidegger, Nietzsche was merely an antimetaphysician. But because he limited himself to denying metaphysics, his own thinking remained in the same dimension as that of traditional metaphysics. Nietzsche did not go beyond metaphysics, but merely ended it.[56]

Thirdly, the "God" also who is conceived as the first physical cause within a series "in itself" is rejected by Heidegger. We have already indicated that such a rejection is entirely justified and need not discuss it here again.

Finally, Heidegger also objects to the affirmation of a "God" who is "lowered" to being the supreme value within a hierarchy of values. He even regards such a view of God as the most pernicious of all. It is a blow in the face of God coming not from unbelievers but precisely from those who believe in Him and their theologians. Such a view is the last desperate convulsion of an enervated metaphysics. It saw the place of God as Be-ing of Supreme Rank occupied first by the absolutized Subject and then by the "Will to Power,"[57] and therefore represented "God" as the Supreme Value. From the standpoint of faith, Heidegger says, this idea is simply blas-

---

54 Heidegger, *ibid.,* p. 235.

55 "Die Stelle, die, metaphysisch gedacht, Gott eignet, ist der Ort der verursachenden Bewirkung und Erhaltung des Seienden als eines Geschaffenen. Dieser Ort Gottes kann leer bleiben." Heidegger, *ibid.,* p. 235.

56 Heidegger, *ibid.,* p. 200.

57 Heidegger, *ibid.,* p. 235.

phemous,[58] for, by conceiving God as a value, it made God subject to man's evaluation.[59] This "God" must be rejected, and for this reason "God"-less thinking brings man closer to the true God.

Heidegger and Theology

The question must also be asked what Heidegger himself thinks about the authentic "affirmation" of the true God. Is this "affirmation" within the reach of philosophy or does it presuppose faith, so that it can be discussed only within the framework of theology, understood as thinking and speaking of man's believing existence?

This question cannot be answered by referring to Heidegger's ideas concerning authentic thinking about the sacred. For, according to him, thinking of the sacred merely is the road toward the eventual "affirmation" of God; it merely is a preparation for the coming of God the Unknown and is not the "affirmation" itself of God. The point at stake is whether in Heidegger's eyes this "affirmation" itself is possible for philosophy. When we speak of God in this connection, the term does not refer to the God to whom man can pray and offer sacrifice, the God for whom he can fall on his knees, play music or dance. That God is the God of Christian revelation. Evidently, the poverty of philosophy cannot "affirm" the wealth of the God who has revealed Himself as Father. What we are concerned with here, however, is the possibility for philosophy to "affirm" God in its own

---

58 "Der letzte Schlag gegen Gott und gegen die übersinnliche Welt besteht darin, dass Gott, das Seiende des Seienden, zum höchsten Wert herabgewürdigt wird . . . Denn dieser Schlag kommt gerade nicht von den Herumstehern, die nicht an Gott glauben, sondern von den Gläubigen und deren Theologen." Heidegger, *ibid.,* pp. 239-240.

59 "Alles Werten ist, auch wo es positiv wertet, eine Subjektivierung." Heidegger, *Ueber den Humanismus,* p. 35.

wretched way, which nonetheless is indispensable for anyone who as man, as a rational being, wants to enter or
remain in the realm of revelation.

Heidegger has always tried to keep his philosophy free
from affirmations borrowed from Christian theology.[60]
He thinks, and correctly so, that in the past philosophy
has not, or at least not sufficiently, been free from it. His
criticism, however, does not mean, as K. Roessing
claims, that he rejects theology.[61] Heidegger merely
wants to emphasize that philosophy is philosophy and not
theology. By theology in this context he does not mean
metaphysics in its second phase but the voice of Christian
existence, that is, Christian theology.

Heidegger, however, has serious reservations with respect to this Christian theology. In this theology the central position is occupied by the idea of creation.[62] In its
development of this idea Christian theology has assimi-
lated philosophical data of Platonic[63] and Aristotelian[64]
origin. It makes God the Supreme Be-ing and the First
Cause of all be-ings. God, then, has not entered philosophy by way of Christian theology, for He was already
present in it on the basis of the proper character of
metaphysics. Precisely on the basis of this character, on
the basis of the fact that metaphysics had its own mode
of thinking, its representation of God "harmonized"
with Christian theology. Precisely for this reason Christian theology was able to assimilate metaphysical ele-

---

[60] Heidegger, *Sein und Zeit*, p. 230.

[61] K. H. Roessing, *Martin Heidegger als godsdienstwijsgeer*,
Assen, 1956, p. 149.

[62] Heidegger, *Einführung in die Metaphysik*, p. 5.

[63] Heidegger, *Platons Lehre von der Wahrheit*, Bern 1947, p. 48.

[64] Heidegger, *Was ist Metaphysik ?*, p. 19.

ments of Plato and Aristotle[65] and to regard the great Greek philosophers as not fully developed Christian theologians.[66]

This seemingly "harmless" critique is in reality an annihilating attack on Christian theology. On the basis of metaphysics' own character, Heidegger says, the God of metaphysics "harmonized" perfectly with Christian theology. The proper character of metaphysics is, as we have seen, its forgetfulness of being. The fact, therefore, that the God of metaphysics could so easily be mastered by theology means that, for Heidegger, theology itself is likewise infected with forgetfulness of being. If Heidegger wants to keep Christian theology away from his philosophy, the reason is not only that philosophy is philosophy but also and especially that Christian theology dwells in forgetfulness of being, stands in the natural attitude. Christian theology does not think in the climate of authentic thinking[67] because it has never made the being of *Dasein* an ontological question.[68]

---

[65] "Der theologische Charakter der Ontologie beruht somit nicht darauf, dass die griechische Metaphysik später von der kirchlichen Theologie des Christentums aufgenommen und durch diese umgebildet wurde. Er beruht vielmehr in der Art, wie sich von früh an das Seiende als das Seiende entborgen hat. Diese Unverborgenheit des Seienden gab erst die Möglichkeit, dass sich die Christliche Theologie der Griechischen Philosophie bemächtigte." Heidegger, *ibid.*, pp. 19-20.

[66] Heidegger, *Einführung in die Metaphysik*, p. 97.

[67] "Eine weltanschauliche, d.h. immer populär ontische Stellungnahme und erst recht jede theologische kommt als solche - sie mag zustimmen oder ablehnen - überhaupt nicht in die Dimension des Problems einer Metaphysik des Daseins." Heidegger, *Kant und das Problem der Metaphysik*, p. 214.

[68] "Die Idee der 'Transzendenz', dass der Mensch etwas sei, das über sich hinauslangt, hat ihre Wurzeln in der christlichen Dogmatik, von der man nicht wird sagen wollen, dass sie das Sein des Menschen je ontologisch zum Problem gemacht hätte." Heidegger, *Sein und Zeit*, p. 49.

All kinds of accusations addressed to Christian theology appear in a new light when they are viewed in this way. Heidegger reproaches theology for having wanted to be a "world view" for its adherents[69] and to take its place among the sciences.[70] This desire is a sign for him that Christian theology also dwells in forgetfulness of being and stands in the natural attitude. Heidegger, in other words, seems to say that not only metaphysics but also Christian theology is by its very nature unable to make an authentic "affirmation" of God.

It would be wrong, however, to conclude that for Heidegger every "affirmation" of God is marked by forgetfulness of being. In faith an authentic "affirmation" of God is possible, for faith does not represent God as the First Cause.[71] Faith therefore also offers a basis upon which an authentic theology can be built.[72] Heidegger conceives that kind of theology as a questioning and thinking reflection upon Christian existence in faith.[73] The security offered by faith, however, is a very special way of "standing" in the truth. If theologians want to express this way of standing in the truth by appealing to philosophy or by adapting theology through philosophy to the fashion of the times, they disregard the sublime charac-

---

[69] Heidegger, *Holzwege,* p. 70.

[70] Heidegger, *Sein und Zeit,* pp. 10, 248.

[71] "Gott wird in der Theologie, nicht im Glauben, als *causa prima,* als die erste Ursache, vorgestellt." Heidegger, *Vorträge und Aufsätze,* p. 50.

[72] "Darum ist eine Auseinandersetzung mit dem Christentum keineswegs und unbedingt eine Bekämpfung des Christlichen, so wenig wie eine Kritik der Theologie schon eine Kritik des Glaubens ist, dessen Auslegung die Theologie sein sollte." Heidegger, *Holzwege,* p. 203.

[73] "Zwar gibt es eine denkende fragende Durcharbeitung der christlich erfahrenen Welt, d.h. des Glaubens. Das ist dann Theologie." Heidegger, *Einführung in die Metaphysik,* p. 6.

185

ter of their task.[74] For the original Christian faith philosophy was foolishness, St. Paul has said, and his warning should not be disregarded by the theologians.[75]

These words show the respect and reverence Heidegger has for authentic theological thinking.[76] They have, however, also a reverse side, for Heidegger thinks that anyone who has entered the realm of faith is no longer able to make the questions of philosophy his own. He may, of course, try to take part in this questioning, he may try to pretend that he seeks authentically, but authentic philosophizing really presupposes that he give up the faith.[77] A so-called "Christian philosophy" is for Heidegger "an iron piece of wood and a misunderstanding."[78]

The Possibility of a Philosophical "Affirmation" of God

We do not want to enter here into a discussion regarding the "definition" of Christian philosophy or choose between the various views about the possibility of authentic philosophizing by a believer. We merely observe that Heidegger has a certain view and may add that he can hardly establish the truth of his view by simply repeating in a single paragraph what one of the competing opinions about this question thinks of it.[79] The question, however, that imposes itself all the more forcefully is whether or not Heidegger regards it possible for philosophy to "affirm" God and not merely to prepare the way for such an "affirmation."

---

[74] Heidegger, *ibid.*, p. 6.

[75] Heidegger, *Was ist Metaphysik ?*, p. 20.

[76] Max Müller, *Existenzphilosophie im geistigen Leben der Gegenwart*, p. 72.

[77] Heidegger, *Einführung in die Metaphysik*, p. 5.

[78] Heidegger, *ibid.*, p. 6.

[79] Cf. the critique of Heidegger's *Einführung in die Metaphysik* by Max Müller, *Universitas*, 1954, pp. 409-413.

In our opinion this question can be answered only by investigating how Heidegger as a philosopher "ultimately" thinks about man. The term "ultimately" is sometimes objected to on the ground that it is meaningless with respect to philosophy in general and to Heidegger in particular because he has not yet spoken his last word. This objection, however, is not unqualifiedly pertinent because in the case of a great philosopher his "first chapter" is crucial and decisive for his entire philosophy, the "final chapter" included, even if this last chapter would never be written. The question, then, is, Does Heidegger want to say that *Dasein* is nothing but man's bringing about of the truth of the *world*, that the being of the existent subject is nothing but his being in the world? If the reply is in the affirmative, then the "affirmation" which the existent subject as "functioning intentionality" himself is will have no other dimension than the world; consequently, the "affirmation" of God, "understood" as "affirmation" of the Transcendent Absolute, would be in principle impossible.

Heidegger has given us extensive descriptions of *Dasein* as the transcending of "cosmic be-ing in *Dasein*." By virtue of this transcending of "cosmic be-ing," *Dasein* can relate to itself and to meaning, it is for itself and meaning is for *Dasein*.[80] That man is for himself means that he is a subject. But the being of the subject is not a being-isolated or being-separated but a being in the world.[81]

When Heidegger makes all these statements about *Dasein*, he wants to speak about man's essence, about

---

[80] "Das Dasein ist nun aber ein Seiendes, das nicht nur inmitten von Seiendem sich befindet, sondern auch *zu* Seiendem und damit auch zu ihm selbst *sich verhält*." Heidegger, *Vom Wesen des Grundes,* p. 47.

[81] "Im Ich-sagen spricht sich das Dasein als In-der-Welt-sein aus." Heidegger, *Sein und Zeit,* p. 321.

that which makes man a man and not something else. Nowhere, however, and we repeat, nowhere does Heidegger say or insinuate that these statements exhaust the essence of man. Consequently, it would be wrong to represent matters as if Heidegger did make any such claim. Roessing thinks that, in describing the being of man as a being in the world, Heidegger wants to say at the same time that "what is not of the world *is* not."[82] Heidegger not only does not want to say this but explicitly says the opposite. He explicitly remarks that the ontological interpretation of being in the world decides neither positively nor negatively about man's possible being toward God. Man's being in the world provides the ground upon which the question about man's relationship to God can be raised.[83]

One could ask whether such a possible relationship to God becomes not illusory if it is accepted that being in the world has no "higher instance" above itself than death.[84] Roessing likewise regards Heidegger's theory about death as an indication that he does not recognize any "higher world."[85] This conclusion, however, is not valid. One can readily grant Heidegger that for being in the world the "highest instance" is death. The question that matters here, however, is whether or not man is encompassed by his being in the world. If the being of man

---

[82] "If 'egoity' is formed by the movement of transcendence itself and this same movement established the world at the same time, then whatever is can be understood only within the unity of 'egoity' and the world. In that case access to the world of being (*Welteingang*) is indeed refused to a transcendent because it can never be taken up in the existential-ontological movement. 'That which is not of the world *is* not' appears to be the tendency of Heidegger's idea of transcendence." Roessing, *op. cit.,* p. 174.

[83] Heidegger, *Vom Wesen des Grundes,* p. 39, note 56.

[84] "Hat das In-der-Welt-sein eine höhere Instanz seines Seinkönnens als seinen Tod ?" Heidegger, *Sein und Zeit,* p. 313.

[85] Roessing, *op. cit.,* p. 149.

would have to be called also a "being over and beyond the world," death would still remain the "highest instance" for his being in the world but not for his integral being-man. Nowhere does Heidegger suggest that being-man is exhausted by being in the world. Nowhere, therefore, does he exclude that the subject-as-*Cogito*, understood as "functioning intentionality," is the "affirming" of the Transcendent Absolute.

Heidegger has never explicitly considered this aspect of the existent subject-as-*Cogito* because he wanted first to prepare the only ground on which authentic affirmations are possible. This ground needed to be cultivated anew because it had been forgotten and deformed in the history of man's thinking. For this reason he rejects also a particular form of thinking about the Transcendent Absolute, viz., the way that is clearly marked by the forgetfulness of being proper to the natural attitude and to scientism.

Heidegger's entire attention is fully occupied with re-establishing this authentic ground of thinking. Authentic thinking has again to see the subject and the worldly meaning as the unity of reciprocal implication, with all the wealth of ideas contained in that implication. One who realizes the necessity of this "step back" and makes the phenomenological reduction in his thinking prefers not to speak *directly* of God.[86] For this reason also thinking about being and about the sacred, as a preparation for "thinking" about God, is not directly for Heidegger a form of theistic thinking. Such thinking is neither theistic nor atheistic. This "neutrality" does not mean that Heidegger is indifferent to the theistic or the atheistic charac-

---

[86] "Wer die Theologie, sowohl diejenige des christlichen Glaubens als auch diejenige der Philosophie, aus gewachsener Herkunft erfahren hat, zieht es heute vor, im Bereich des Denkens von Gott zu schweigen." Heidegger, *Identität und Differenz,* p. 51.

ter of his thinking,[87] or that an eventual "affirmation" of God is an act of faith. It means merely that in the restoration of authentic thinking, in reflecting upon the reciprocal implication of subject and wordly meaning, God cannot be directly discussed because, as Transcendent, God does not let Himself be encountered like a worldly meaning.[88] Man cannot experience God just as he experiences the world.

---

[87] "Doch mit diesem Hinweis möchte sich das Denken, das in die Wahrheit des Seins als das Zu-denkende vorweist, keineswegs für den Theismus entschieden haben. Theistisch kann es so wenig sein wie atheistisch. Dies aber nicht auf Grund einer gleichgültigen Haltung, sondern aus der Achtung der Grenzen, die dem Denken als Denken gesetzt sind und zwar durch das, was sich ihm als das Zu-denkende gibt, durch die Wahrheit des Seins." Heidegger, *Ueber den Humanismus*, p. 37.

[88] Müller, *Existenzphilosophie im geistigen Leben der Gegenwart*, pp. 73-74.

EPILOGUE

The preceding considerations have led us to the conclusion that a philosophy which really endeavors to think in a radical way cannot escape the question regarding meaning as meaning. This question imposes itself irresistibly—to such an extent that its very rejection as a legitimate question re-affirms its inevitable character. In the past, however, the question of meaning used to be raised in the context of representative realism. The climate of phenomenological thinking, on the other hand, is determined by intentionality and the phenomenological reduction, which imply the denial of representative realism. For this reason some metaphysicians think that phenomenology neither is nor can be a metaphysics. Representative realism itself, however, has been exposed by phenomenology as implying an internal contradiction, so that a metaphysics of the representative type is an impossibility.

The "Affirmation" of Transcendent Being

It is a mistake to think that phenomenology cannot ask about meaning as meaning because it cannot ask this question in the context of representative realism. The inspiration of traditional metaphysics, that is, the radicalism of its thinking, harmonizes very well with phenomenological realism. A metaphysics of the phenomenologically realistic type asks about be-ing as be-ing, about meaning as meaning, within the context of intentionality and the phenomenological reduction. Within that context

191

be-ing manifests itself as "caused." Hence the question of "why," understood as asking about the "cause," must be raised because the "Cause" is actually already "affirmed" in an implicit way as soon as be-ing as be-ing is affirmed.

It does not make sense to refuse to ask this question on the pretext that traditional metaphysics has replied to it from the natural attitude and was thus induced to seek a first "Cause"-in-Itself. Not even the fact that some forms of metaphysical thinking went so far as to conceive the "First Cause" as first within a series justifies anyone to reject each and every form of "affirming" a "First Cause" as contradictory. The "First Cause" of be-ing is the Transcendent Being. The "affirmation" of the Transcendent Being does not imply that be-ing is henceforth affirmed by the subject from the standpoint of the Absolute. The "affirmation" of the Transcendent Being is directly nothing but the affirmation of the implications of be-ing. The existent subject-as-*Cogito* himself is the "always active" affirmation of be-ing, but this be-ing reveals itself as pointing to the Transcendent Being. Thus the existent subject-as-*Cogito* is, as the direct affirmation of be-ing, equiprimordially also the indirect "affirmation" of the Transcendent Being.

The "Speaking Word"

The indirect character of the "affirmation" of the Transcendent Being has consequences with respect to the "names" which metaphysics gives to the Transcendent Being. We have repeatedly stressed how circumspect and careful metaphysics must be before it can commit itself to saying that God "is." For the term "is" is used in reference to be-ing, and God "is" not a be-ing. Even this statement is hardly more than empty words for one who does not become personally involved in the questioning proper to metaphysics. Only by personal involvement in the searching of metaphysics does man see what possibilities of affirmation he has and which affirmations he must make without being able to make them *as* they ought to be made. We have mentioned above the indirect and "directional" character of all terms used to "affirm" the Being of God. One who does not keep this character constantly in mind does not realize that the concepts he uses are degenerated by the very use he makes of them.

Generally speaking, this kind of degeneration can be prevented only if philosophers and theologians ceaselessly try to keep alive the sense of the terms which they use. As soon as the "spoken word" is at the disposal of a speaking community as a kind of "thing," the origin and the life of a word begins to disappear and there is danger that gradually nothing will remain of it but a lifeless term. The origin of the word is real speech, the "speaking word," which is called "real" because it voices reality. Reality is conceptualized in speaking, and the concept is embodied in language. The word is intentional, it is essentially a pointer to something which it itself is not, to a reality which is "worded" in a personal act of "seeing." This act is a personal act because it is man *himself* who "sees." If he *himself* does not see, then he does not *see*.

If the origin of the word that has been spoken is not kept alive by a personal following of the word's intentionality, the word begins to lead a kind of isolated existence. It becomes, as it were, reified, it is at the service of a speaking community like a utensil and they use it without *really* saying anything. Such a use of words is, in Heidegger's language, "talk."[1] It is hardly more than

---

[1] "Man versteht nicht so sehr das beredete Seiende, sondern man hört schon nur auf das Geredete als solches." Heidegger, *Sein und Zeit*, p. 168.

empty verbiage. The immediate result is that one no longer realizes that every word referring to man and anything human can have an endless variety of senses. I can say that man is a subject, I can speak of love and of sin, but what does it mean if I do not *see* that what these words express can be realized in an endless variety of different ways?[2] With respect to man and anything human all terms are analogous terms. Yet my awareness of this analogous character fades away when I manipulate "spoken words."

The "Names" of God and "Speaking"

If it is true that every word has a "directional" value and points to something which it is not, the same is true in a double sense with respect to the "names" used to refer to God. God is not a present presence for man, He is not a datum of man's experience. Hence man does not have any terms indicating concepts that directly say what God is. The philosopher therefore has to make use of terms embodying an understanding that is directly concerned, not with God, but with a reality which man can experience. Reality itself compels man to a mode of "affirming" that transcends his direct affirmations. If that which compels man to go beyond his direct affirmations were not the fact that the directly affirmed reality *itself* points "over and beyond" itself, then all the indirect affirmations which man's metaphysical reflection upon reality compels him to make would be nothing else but projections.

One who realizes that the indirect "affirmation" of God is not a projection of man's own mind should never lose sight of the fact that his "affirmation" is and remains in-

---

[2] Dondeyne, "L'athéisme contemporain et le problème des attributs de Dieu," *Foi et réflexion philosophique,* Louvain, 1961, pp. 472-475.

direct. The word spoken by man is intentional and points to the reality expressed by it. Within this intentionality no form of speaking can be said to be a speaking about God. Compelled by his metaphysical consciousness, however, man uses the intentionality of his words to express a "pointing" of reality *itself* to God. It remains true, of course, that his words themselves do not thereby acquire an intentionality which transcends their reference to present, perceptible reality. When man gives "names" to God, these words do not reach God as a present reality. They do not "dwell" with God in the way man's speaking about perceptible reality "dwells" with reality. Nevertheless, man has to speak because his metaphysical reflection upon reality itself compels him. This means that he *has to* speak inadequately because he does not have any other concepts than those with which he speaks about perceptible reality. His speaking about God is and remains indirect and a "pointing to," and is therefore analogous in a second sense.

All speaking finds its ultimate form in the judgment. However, when one looks at the formulated judgment about God, the indirect and "pointing" character of man's speaking about God is no longer "visible." The judgment, "God 'is'" can be correctly understood only if I realize the implications of the metaphysical consciousness upon which this judgment is based. It can be correctly understood only if it is seen in the light of a metaphysical "speaking word." Only in this light does one see that to every positive judgment about God a negative judgment must at once be added. This negative judgment must make it clear that metaphysical consciousness does not add a new dimension to the intentionality of speech as if man's speaking about God could ever be adequate. Man's speaking about God makes use of the intentionality of the human word which refers to perceptible reality and therefore must always be followed by a negation.

One who realizes that the "speaking word" easily degenerates into "talk" (*Gerede*) will have little difficulty in understanding that the same tendency to degeneration affects man's speaking about God even more strongly. This degeneration begins when, after recognizing the necessity to add a negative judgment to every positive judgment, one neglects to do so on the ground that it is sufficient to recognize that necessity in principle. The omission of those negative judgments means that *de facto* only positive judgments remain. There is then great danger that the necessity to add a negative judgment to every positive statement about God will be forgotten. As soon as the necessity is forgotten, there is no longer any awareness that all "names" of God have merely a "directional" character, and ultimately one will think that one really "knows" what one is speaking about with respect to God. The stage is then laid for manipulating His "names" as one can manipulate the "clear and distinct ideas" of mathematics.[3]

Above we have said that under "certain conditions" the "primitive fact" of existential phenomenology and the "inspiration" of traditional metaphysics can be harmonized. *Both* sides therefore may and must stipulate certain conditions. We have endeavored to formulate these conditions as clearly as possible and to indicate why they must be made. Personally I would regret it very much if a difference of opinion would split my fellow philosophers into two warring factions, especially because that difference is perhaps largely based upon a misunderstanding of what the two *really* want to affirm.

---

[3] Dondeyne, *ibid.,* p. 472.

INDEX OF NAMES

INDEX OF SUBJECT MATTER

Absolute, 25 ff.; metaphysics and the, 25 ff., 156 ff.; the Transcendent, 27, 30, 156 f.; as the "absolutized," 30 ff.; rejected to save the "metaphysical," 33 ff., 134, 157 ff.; apex of traditional metaphysics, 133 f.; phenomenology and rejection of, 33 ff., 134; as Truth itself and Goodness itself, 161 ff.

Affirmation, of the Absolute, 133 f.; in negation, 20 ff.; of God, 141 ff., 150 f., 177 ff., 182 ff.; of Creator, 152 ff.; philosophical of God, 186 ff.; of Transcendent Being, 191 ff.

Appearance, be-ing and, 18, 62 f.

Being, be-ing and, XII, 77 ff., 89 ff., 150; not an empty word, 14; Transcendent, 27 f., see also *God;* in itself and for us, 58 ff., 80, 103 ff., 116 ff., 122 ff., 149 ff.; forgetfulness of, see *Forgetfulness;* metaphysics and, 76 ff.; no-thingness and, 80 ff.; dread and, 84 ff.; truth and, 78 ff.; "occurrence" of, 93 f.; is not God, 96 ff.; autonomy of, 120 ff.; as "initiative," 166 ff.; "mission" of, 166 ff.; affirmation of Transcendent, 191 ff.

Be-ing, being and, XII, 77 ff., 89 ff., 150; problem of, 18 f.; universality of, 24 f.; appearing, 62; man as "response" to, 69 ff.; the why of, 135 ff., see also *Cause;* meaning and, 141; other than, 82 f., 150 ff.; and affirmation of Creator, 152 ff.

Causality, principle of, 176 ff. See also *Cause.*

Cause, Absolute, 28 f.; contingency and, 42 ff.; efficient, 136; of be-ing, 134 ff., 141 ff., 144 ff.; the term, 146 ff.

Cogito, the Cartesian, 59.

Contingency, subject's, 41, 158; theology and, 42 ff.; two senses of, 159 ff.

Creator, affirmation of, 152 ff.; causality and, 42 ff., 158 ff.

Dasein, as source of thinking, 68 ff.; no-thingness and, 82 ff.; disclosure of, 94 f.; world and, 123 f.

Doubt, Cartesian, 59.

Dread, be-ing and, 84 ff.

Encounter, knowledge as, 103 ff.; meaning as term of, 120 ff.

Essentialism of scholastic metaphysics, 108 ff., 117 ff.

Ethics, realism and, 112 f.; metaphysics and, 176.

Existentialism, 49. See also *Phenomenology.*

Faith as affirmation of God, 185 f.

Forgetfulness of being, 66 f., 78 ff., 88, 92 ff., 107 ff., 119, 132, 136, 167 ff.

God, as Absolute, 27 ff.; inevitable "doctrine" of, 31 ff.; contingency and, 42 ff.; being is not, 96 ff.; affirmation of, 141 ff., 150 f., 177 ff., 182 ff.; as Other than be-ing, 150 ff.; proofs for existence of, 165 ff., 179 ff.; as value, 181 f.; philosophical affirmation of, 186 ff.; names of, 194 ff.

Goodness, the Absolute as Goodness itself, 161 ff.

INDEX OF SUBJECT MATTER

INDEX OF SUBJECT MATTER